"This book brings information that is desperately needed
to open hearts and homes to some of God's little ones."
Pat Palau
The Luis Palau Evangelistic Association

"A book full of loving kindness and practical knowledge
and experience . . . an immense contribution
to the love-thirsting orphans and homes expecting
to adopt children around the world."
Ling and Yang Zhang
Chinese Writers and Translators

"Few issues touch my heart like adoption.
I pray that this book will be used by God
to touch your heart as well.
Jorie has woven together a powerful and practical guide
for those interested in this vital subject."
Dennis Rainey
Family Life Today

"This book provides a rich resource of information
and practical advice to all who are interested in adopting children
from other countries. I hope that it will encourage many more people
to bring new life and hope to children who might otherwise
be doomed to lives of misery."
Baroness Caroline Cox
Deputy Speaker, British House of Lords
President, Christian Solidarity International, U.K.

P9-DFS-117

ADOPTING
for GOOD

A Guide
for People
Considering
Adoption

Jorie Kincaid

InterVarsity Press
Downers Grove, Illinois

InterVarsity Press® is the book-publishing division of InterVarsity Christian Fellowship®, a student movement active on campus at hundreds of universities, colleges and schools of nursing in the United States of America, and a member movement of the International Fellowship of Evangelical Students. For information about local and regional activities, write Public Relations Dept., InterVarsity Christian Fellowship, 6400 Schroeder Rd., P.O. Box 7895, Madison, WI 53707-7895.

All Scripture quotations, unless otherwise indicated, are taken from the HOLY BIBLE, NEW INTERNATIONAL VERSION®. NIV®. Copyright ©1973, 1978, 1984 by International Bible Society. Used by permission of Zondervan Publishing House. All rights reserved.

Cover photograph: Penny Gentieu/Tony Stone Images

ISBN 0-8308-1970-3

Printed in the United States of America ⊗

Library of Congress Cataloging-in-Publication Data

Kincaid, Jorie.

    Adopting for good/Jorie Kincaid.

       p.   cm.

    Includes bibliographical references.

    ISBN 0-8308-1970-3 (alk. paper)

     1. Adoption   2. Adoption—Religious aspects—Christianity.

  I. Title

  HV875.K47   1997

  362.73'4—dc21   97-33698
                                                                          CIP

15	14	13	12	11	10	9	8	7	6	5	4	3	2	1
08	07	06	05	04	03	02	01	00	99	98	97			

To my mom, Anna Hultgren, and to the memory of my dad,
Arne Hultgren, who ignited the passion I feel for children who need parents.

To my husband, Ron, who encouraged me to be a voice for those
children who cannot speak on behalf of themselves.

To my children, Tad, David, Luke, Joel, Mark, Andrea and
Cam Kincaid, who I pray will carry on this passion for needy children
and pass it on to their children.

And to children the world over who still wait for parents—
that they **all** might find them.

"If you spend yourselves in behalf of the hungry
and satisfy the needs of the oppressed,
then your light will rise in the darkness,
and your night will become like the noonday."
Isaiah 58:10

Acknowledgments

How did a mother of seven write a book? Because her husband shouldered her responsibilities at home in order to give her time to think and write. Because her children helped with cooking and babysitting and did not complain even when they had no clean socks. Because she was the recipient of a freezerful of meals, child care and countless prayers from her church family. Thank you, Ron, for suggesting that I write this book and for providing the time for me to do so. Thank you, Cindy Bunch-Hotaling, editor at IVP, for sharing my passion for adoption and for helping birth the ideas for this book. Thanks to my children, Tad, David, Luke, Joel, Mark, Andrea and Cam, for the prayers, hugs, milk shakes and special breakfasts you made for me when I was writing. Thank you, Marietta Johanns, for praying and cooking incessantly on my behalf. Thank you, Judy Curtis, Sherri Wells and Amber Sorenson, my special team of coworkers who took portions of my Orphans Overseas work so that I could concentrate on writing. Thank you, Robert Jaquiss, for researching statistics for me on your computer, often late into the night. And thank you to the many families who graciously allowed me to use their personal experiences to encourage others. Because of you all, it is my prayer that countless children who need parents will have the privilege of being adopted.

1

IGNITING A PASSION FOR ADOPTION

Religion that God our Father accepts as pure and faultless
is this: to look after orphans and widows
in their distress and to keep oneself from being
polluted by the world.
JAMES 1:27

WITHOUT WARNING, EIGHT WEEKS INTO HER PREGNANCY, Taylor began vomiting uncontrollably. Many hours later, weakened and dehydrated, she was admitted to the emergency room, initiating a regimen of intravenous feeding tubes, medication and bed rest that were to be her companions for the rest of her pregnancy.

Though she was soon permitted to come home, her plan to finish a project for her master's degree during leisurely months of pregnancy evaporated. She was confined to her bed, constantly hooked up to an intravenous line for nourishment and fluids, since she was unable to keep even water down without vomiting. Days drifted into nights as Taylor fought the effects of medication. Her husband, Brad, and her extended family cared for her month after month, fearful for her and her unborn baby. Countless times in her agonizing existence it was only the hope of one day holding her precious baby that helped her endure.

Yet that hope never materialized. At seven months she and Brad returned to the hospital, this time to deliver their stillborn baby, Seth, who died *in utero* of causes apparently unrelated to her own difficulties. They held the baby for whom they had given so much emotional and physical energy, and they wept for themselves, for him and for the relationship that was stolen before they even had a chance to introduce themselves.

Taylor and Brad struggled in the months following Seth's death. Although busy with her master's project, Taylor was at home and was able to take time to grieve. She began to look forward to another child, possibly through adoption. Although she was not infertile, no one knew what another pregnancy would hold for her. Brad buried himself and his feelings in his job, declaring that he did not want any more children. Taylor realized her hopes for adoption needed to be tabled at least until things were sorted out. Their marriage faltered under the stress.

Unwilling to lose each other, they participated in many months of counseling; Brad did the grieving he had previously avoided. After counseling had given him the chance to make peace with his feelings, he decided he was ready to adopt a baby.

A Child Has Arrived!

Imagine the anticipation those of us who know them experienced six months later when the plane carrying Taylor, Brad and their newly adopted daughter, Lauren, taxied up to the gate. Grandparents, extended family and friends stood laden with video cameras and still cameras, helium balloons, wrapped packages, cries of welcome and freely flowing tears as the new family made their entry into the world of people who loved them.

What a difference adoption has made in their lives! Overnight Taylor and Brad were catapulted into a world of diapers and bottles, baby clothes and night lights, mobiles and music boxes, as well as the incomparable joy of sharing love and nurture with an eight-pound newborn who needed parents. Are they fortunate? Of course! Is Lauren a lucky baby? Certainly! Do they love her as much as they would have loved Seth? Yes! They have said that they cannot imagine loving any other child more than they love their Lauren. Adoption is a tremendous solution for families who long for children and for children who need parents.

Were Taylor and Brad nervous about adoption? Yes, of course they were. They dreaded the intrusive paperwork they knew accompanied adoption as well the home study that had to be accomplished. As a young couple, they were concerned about the expenses of adoption. They feared the potentially long wait they heard could be involved. Having lost a baby of their own, they were especially worried about this baby's health. And, probably most of all, they protected their feelings even as they boarded the plane to pick their baby up and drove from the airport to the hospital in which she was being cared for. After all, they had dared to love before and been burned. They both admit they were a little afraid to bare their emotions to love again.

But their fears dispersed as soon as they laid eyes on Lauren, who was tiny and delicate and beautiful. They both were smitten with love toward this treasure which God had entrusted to them. They look forward to someday adopting another child as well.

The Story Is Repeated
Visualize the ecstasy—and exhaustion—a single adoptive mom felt as she set eyes on her daughter, Betsy, for the first

time after experiencing an eleven-hour plane ride and fourteen-hour train ride to reach her daughter's orphanage. Was it worth the effort? She wept tears of delight, realizing that, though she had not had the privilege of marriage and biological children as she had thought she would, still she had the privilege of becoming a mother to this tiny, sweet, crying little girl who otherwise faced life in an orphanage. Betsy is now the joy of her life (and, remarkably, looks just like her adoptive mom!). Through adoption, her dream of parenting has become reality.

Another family with two biological boys yearned for the experience of parenting a little girl. They did not imagine that adopting one would ever be a possibility for them. But when they realized that baby girls around the world needed homes, they shared their heartfelt desire with their extended family, and the family helped them gather the money necessary for the adoption.

The mother finds delight in sewing mother-daughter dresses and feminine outfits for her little girl, Alexandra, and the father surprises them all by shopping for little-girl clothes for the daughter he claims took three seconds to bond with at the airport! And how is Alexandra, who is adored by two big brothers, different than if she had not been adopted? Her life is immensely different, full of opportunities otherwise unavailable to her. This whole family is enriched by adoption.

For those who have enough love in their hearts to share with a child who needs parents, adoption is a wonderful way to create or to build a family. In my work with Orphans Overseas, I have excitedly anticipated the arrivals of dozens of adoptive families at airports or in hospital corridors, never feeling anything less than amazement over the miracle of joy that adoption brings.

A Personal Passion

As an adopted child myself, I have lived with the reality of adoption every day of my life. I owe my life to a woman of whom I've never seen a picture. Neither do I know her name. I can summarize my family background information in less than a paragraph. My birth mother was an eighteen-year-old college student when she became pregnant with me. My birth father was a married man with children, making their relationship one that should not have been. But it was, and I was born, and that's reality in our world.

I do not know who was there for my birth mother when she found out she was pregnant. I assume she was afraid, perhaps alone, perhaps feeling morning sickness when she was making decisions regarding my future. Was I to live or die? And if I lived, who would be my parents? I don't know whether my birth father even knew of her condition, or whether anyone guided her into her courageous decision to go through what had to be an unplanned, inconvenient pregnancy and consequent placement of me in an adoptive family. She may have faced great humiliation to herself and shame to her family in order to give me my physical life. I know that it took an amazing amount of courage to make the choices she made on my behalf.

I am grateful. My experience as an adopted child was a great one. I experienced first-hand the love of a mom and dad who adored me and loved to tell me the story of my birth mother who "loved me so much that she wanted to give me more than she was able to provide." I never tired of hearing the circumstances of my adoption, and my mom never seemed to tire of responding to my request, "Tell me about my birth mom." Just as I owe my physical life to my birth mother, I owe my spiritual life to my mom and dad who taught me about the God of the universe who created me and loved me enough to die for me, giving me a sense of worth and healthy self-esteem—who loved me with a love that engulfed my past circumstances and did not depend of my performance.

It is largely due to my positive experience as an adopted child that I have such a passion today for orphan children. After the birth of our four sons, Tad, David, Luke and Joel, stair-stepped in height and all bearing a distinct family resemblance, my husband and I decided we would like to have the experience of adopting a child, since my experience with adoption had been so good. Our fifth son, Mark, joined us ten months later, a domestic adoption. Eighteen months later we had the privilege of adopting our first daughter, Andrea, one of the early adoptions following the death of a totalitarian dictator in Eastern Europe. Last year on Christmas day our second daughter, Cam, was born in Asia and soon joined us in Oregon.

My husband, Ron, and I will carry forever in our minds the vivid memories of hundreds of children with arms reaching out to us—the ones we had to leave behind. We began an adoption ministry early in 1991, called Orphans Overseas, whose mission statement declares that we seek to honor Christ by serving the needs of orphans worldwide. The members of the board of directors believed that even if it were possible to help only one orphan, the time and money invested would be worth it.

Our nonprofit organization, which became a fully licensed adoption agency in the state of Oregon in 1992, has implemented its mission of serving orphans in four ways: (1) It seeks to supplement government stipends for orphanages in developing countries, providing food, clothing, medicine and other items necessary to insure quality of life for the orphans living there. (2) It seeks to establish sponsorship programs for orphans, linking them with families in the U.S. who will give emotional support by writing to them and providing a small financial stipend for their welfare. (3) It seeks to provide care for single, pregnant women to help ensure a healthy birth. (4)

It seeks to facilitate adoptions for legal orphans, believing that no matter how good we can make the conditions in an orphanage, they simply can't substitute for a loving mother and father. The work of Orphans Overseas has now spread to several countries.

Adoption Misunderstood

In some areas of the world adoption is a controversial topic. It is feared by those who do not understand how a child unrelated by blood can be loved just as much as a biological child. Adoption is mistrusted. Sometimes it is used by the wrong people to achieve monetary gain from the plight of helpless children. Although the material in this book is completely factual, all identities of individuals and countries have been omitted in order to insure the anonymity of individuals who work tirelessly in all corners of the world, sometimes at great risk to themselves, and the innocent children who wait for parents to love them.

In every country in which our organization works, the fear that Americans adopt children to kill them and use their organs for organ banks has preceded our visit. It has been my privilege and passion to educate people all over the world regarding adoption, dispelling myths and fears and helping people to realize that adoption often means the difference between life and death to a child, as well as providing a wonderfully enriching experience for the adoptive parents.

It is my prayer that as a result of this book many more children without parents will find families with arms to snuggle them and voices to tell them they are special. You may have heard that there are no children available to adopt, but this simply is not true. There are thousands of children around the world who wait—sometimes in vain—for parents to love them.

2

FORGOTTEN
CHILDREN

"Lord, when was it that we saw you hungry
and gave you food, or thirsty and gave you
something to drink?"
"Truly I tell you, just as you did it to one of
the least of these who are members of my family,
you did it to me."
MATTHEW 25:37, 40 NRSV

I WILL NEVER FORGET GABRIELLA, A ONE-YEAR-OLD WITH HAUNT-ingly beautiful blue eyes and blond, curly hair. I went over-seas with my husband, Ron, who was visiting a country newly relieved from the oppression of a totalitarian dictator, to see if we could find a little girl who needed a home. The orphanage staff, through our interpreter, declared enthusiastically, "We have a baby for you! You must be her American mother! She has big eyes and blond curly hair like you! You must be her American mother!"

The waiting time between their happy declarations and the doctor's bringing of the baby seemed endless. I felt almost squeamish with worry, yet also dared to maintain hope that perhaps we were going to have the privilege of parenting a daughter along with our five sons.

Eventually the doctor brought the baby, wrapped tightly in

a blanket. I noted that the bundle looked especially small, almost like a newborn, but was distracted from dwelling on her size as soon as her face became visible. Their descriptions were accurate. Gabriella's head was a mass of honey-blond curls, and her enormous blue eyes dominated her tiny face. Her lips curled into just the hint of a smile, and I responded by asking if I could hold her and unwrap her blanket.

No one could have prepared me for the sight of hanging skin and bones, virtually being held together by that blanket which had masked her condition. I couldn't imagine how she mustered the strength from that wasted body even to keep her eyes open, let alone smile. She clearly weighed under ten pounds, and yet she was a year old. Without asking, I just knew she couldn't survive the trip home.

"Why is she dying?" I pleaded.

My interpreter explained in a voice husky with the emotion he obviously felt for this innocent child. Gabriella had been hospitalized three weeks earlier with flulike symptoms. Realizing she had lost weight rapidly, the doctor had ordered high-calorie fresh foods for her—a luxury unknown to many in this economically depressed country. But when the fresh milk, cheese, vegetables and meat had arrived, the hospital staff took them home for their own undernourished children. I struggled to understand a country so poor that a hospital staff would steal food for their own children. There was nothing I could do for her. I handed her back to the doctor.

Did Gabriella die in vain? I like to think not. I vowed never to forget her and the other children like her who wait for mothers and fathers. All over the world children are born to parents who die or are unable to care for them. These are the forgotten children, the children who need parents. It is for these I carry my story.

How Many Gabriellas?

In the last few years the fall of the dictator in Romania, China's practice of limiting the size of families, the break-up of the former Soviet Union, the AIDS epidemic in countries such as Uganda, plus wars and natural disasters, have together produced a staggering number of orphaned children. No country or people is exempt from this problem. No country or people is to be blamed for choices or values that we can't understand without living within the circumstances that prompted those choices or values. But once we are aware of the needs of these forgotten children, we are no longer exempt from blame if we turn our heads and let them remain forgotten.

The orphanage where Gabriella lived was a world of nearly six hundred children who rarely, if ever, ventured beyond those institutional walls. Some had never seen a car. Others had never touched grass. Still others waited all day long in hopes of being picked up. Some rarely merited a clean diaper because orphanage workers had far too many children to tend. Others had flies attached to the encrusted matter around their eyes.

In my own home with seven healthy children, the noise level is sometimes nerve-wracking. In this six-hundred-child orphanage, the silence was many times more nerve-wracking. The few toys they had were attached high up on the walls or behind glass cabinets—for decoration, not for play. Nothing was happening; children did not laugh and play—they sat and looked.

For toddlers in this poverty-stricken institution, mealtime meant waiting in line while an orphanage worker might drop an unadorned steaming-hot potato into their bare little hands. The children would hungrily devour the potato before it even cooled, disregarding the pain. Apparently the prospect of losing that potato to a more aggressive child was more upsetting than a burned tongue and throat.

Across Another Ocean

In other parts of the world people have been employed by hospitals to drown babies who are born to single mothers or who are unwanted because they are believed unable to contribute to the family's livelihood. This reality is perhaps incomprehensible to us (and it should be!), but we can't fathom the reality of living on a $25 monthly wage; we can't imagine needing to depend on our sons to provide for us in our old age instead of on IRAs or 401(k)s.

I can only try to feel the fear a mother in a developing country experiences when she births a baby with a cleft lip and palate and knows she has no means of nursing that baby. What to us in the Western world is a minor, correctable problem is to her baby a death sentence. In this situation she will likely abandon her baby because she feels she has no other choice. In order for her to keep her baby she would need the means to hire a person to feed this child who cannot suck and the means to pay for impossibly expensive surgery.

If this baby is abandoned and no one discovers him or her, the baby will surely die. If the baby in discovered and placed in an orphanage, the orphanage staff will most likely be faced with the decision as to whether the baby will receive half-strength formula, quarter-strength formula or no formula at all. When funds are sharply limited, as they usually are in a developing country, an orphanage worker may make a choice far different than we would want to see made in this or another child's life. The death rate in an orphanage may be very high due to lack of heat and formula, despite a caring staff. The orphanage worker may have to choose to give the formula to the child who has the best chance of survival.

Imagine one orphanage we visited in the dead of winter.

The babies' faces were chapped bright red from the cold. They were wrapped in layers in an attempt to keep them warm, but there was no heat at all in the orphanage. We were told 90 percent of the babies in some of these orphanages die.

Still Another Direction

In another developing country, it is rare to even have a government-run orphanage for children under two years old. The government officials in this country explained to us that, since babies under two need more caregivers, the government is usually unable to provide this kind of social service. What an impossible situation a baby without parents faces here. If extended family is unable to care for that child, the baby will most likely die.

In this same country, if a young woman becomes pregnant before she is married, her family experiences much shame. If the young woman keeps her baby, she is not considered marriageable. Consequently, many of these young women deliver their babies in a hospital and quickly run away. I visited a maternity hospital staff doing its very best to keep an abandoned, premature newborn alive so that he could be placed for adoption. The hospital was a concrete building with outside corridors and, instead of windows, large openings that let in the outside air. The baby was lying on a straw mat on a metal bunk, wrapped in several layers of blankets for warmth. The nurses had also wrapped the baby in a layer of plastic for insulation, trying to combat the unseasonable cold they were experiencing. In addition, the nurses had placed beneath the bunk a single electric cooking burner that glowed orange with heat. Those nurses had little with which to work, but they acted with love and concern for the special needs of that baby. I watched those same nurses cry when a another baby left their care for adoption in the U.S.

Do these caregivers in other countries love the children for whom they care? Often they demonstrate in many tangible ways that they love them very much. But are they able to adequately care for these children? Without outside help, often they cannot.

In still another country ravaged by forty years of totalitarian rule we visited a baby orphanage with broken-down plumbing and at least three feet of raw sewage in the basement. At the request of the orphanage director, our first project was to build an eight-foot wall topped with barbed wire and broken glass surrounding the orphanage. You may wonder why such a project was picked as a priority. The orphanage director explained. When the toddlers went out into the front of the orphanage compound to play, the neighbor children would sneak in and strip the playing orphans naked, in order to take clothes home to their own younger siblings who had nothing to wear!

In another orphanage in this same country we noticed a pretty older girl who was obviously trying her hardest to look like a boy by wearing boyish clothes and rejecting earrings or any sign of femininity. Why? Our guide explained that sometimes older girls are sexually abused by older boys in the orphanage or by caregivers. One orphanage director of an older children's orphanage confided that he had a dream of a job where he "could have [sex with] a different girl every night." Imagine the fear the young girls in that institution feel every night as they lie down to sleep.

Sometimes in orphanages not just food but even water must be rationed; there is not enough pure drinking water. These children experience constant thirst. Many will then drink impure water from wherever they can find it and end up with parasites.

Children who manage to grow up in this kind of institutional setting have very limited prospects for a bright future. Most developing countries will be able to offer only menial positions to young adults as they leave an orphanage—jobs such as street sweeping or nonskilled factory work. In some countries prostitution is a sad but real option for an uneducated, untrained young woman, or drug dealing a tragic alternative for an uneducated, untrained young man. Orphanages often must turn these "children" out on their own by age sixteen out of financial necessity.

Children in the U.S. Without Parents

Although the United States no longer has an orphanage system for children without parents, it is not exempt from the problem of forgotten children. Children who are part of the social welfare system here are in a foster care system. Exact and comprehensive data for this system is somewhat lacking because until now all reporting of statistics by individual states has been voluntary. The Department of Health and Human Services is beginning to implement a new mandatory collection system known as the Adoption and Foster Care Analysis and Reporting System (AFCARS), which will provide much information regarding children in our own child welfare system.

Until the new system is implemented, the statistics can only roughly show trends. In 1994, the national estimate of children in foster care was listed as a staggering 469,073, and this number is rising each year. The average length of stay for a child in foster care is two and one-half years. Though children range in age from birth to 18, the average median age of a child in foster care is 9 years old. An estimated 4 percent of the children are less than 1 year old, with an estimated 31 percent ranging from 1 to 5 years old. Another 35 percent are 6 to 12 years old, and an additional 27 percent are teenagers.

Two percent of the children are between 18 and 19 years old. The ethnicity of children in foster care is 32 percent Caucasian, 47 percent African American, 14 percent Hispanic, 1 percent Asian and 6 percent unknown.[1]

In 1993, 35,000 of the 442,218 children in foster care in the United States were placed in adoptive homes or had their adoptions finalized. Another 21,000 children were available for adoption with no one to adopt them! An additional 30,000 were waiting for legal papers relinquishing them for adoption, and then they too would be waiting for adoptive families. The remaining 356,218 were in foster care either to safeguard them from abuse or neglect or because their parents were in rehabilitation for drug use, alcoholism, prostitution or incarceration, so they were not available for adoption.[2]

In addition, loose sexual standards give the United States the highest incidence in the world of children conceived by unmarried women. Today well over one million births per year in the U.S. are out-of-wedlock births.[3] "Of unmarried mothers today, 49 percent choose abortion, 49 percent keep the child and become single parents, and only 2 percent make adoption plans."[4] Our young women have freedom and the ability to make choices. The babies conceived by them don't have the same choices. Some of these are the forgotten children in the U.S.A.

Many single young women who become pregnant don't want a baby to interfere with their work or school schedule and so will opt for abortion. Of those who do continue their pregnancies and give birth, many are unable to handle the emotional and financial responsibilities of parenting as a single mother. Without a strong support system from extended family or friends, some of these women will end up on welfare. In many cases low self-esteem contributed to the young woman's becoming pregnant. The same low self-esteem can contribute to a lack of confidence to continue in school or to interview for a job, without which welfare is often inevitable.

Although these young mothers may love their babies very much, the frustration they will face from the challenges of parenting a baby without adequate emotional and financial support can be overwhelming, even setting the stage for potential abuse.

Unless we are willing to become involved in the lives of these young women, we are leaving thousands of babies at risk of being forgotten. Am I going to turn my back on these mothers, or am I going to help them? Who is willing to walk alongside of them to help them make wise choices for their own futures, and for the futures of their babies? These women do not need to be blamed for their choices; they need support to help them through a difficult time in their lives. They need people to befriend them, advocate for them and perhaps even house them. Orphans Overseas, for example, operates a maternity residence for women who need emotional and physical help during an unplanned pregnancy and assistance in choosing adoptive families.

What Can We Do?

For a myriad of reasons millions of children in the world will never know the joy of a parent's love unless we choose to become involved. What can we do?

One positive thing we can do is to help raise the quality of life for needy children in the world. There are many reputable relief agencies working with orphan children in numerous countries. The baby orphanage once filled with raw sewage now has plumbing, electricity, back-up generators, playground equipment, a new roof, new decorating and—most important of all—healthy, well-fed, happy children, thanks to people who chose to become involved. The difference is incredible.

As part of our care program for orphanages around the world, Orphans Overseas has provided freezers, clothing, toys, medicines, vitamins, hepatitis-B vaccine for orphans and staff, dental equipment, scabies medicine, water purifiers, formula—even things like sausages, chickens and bananas which children otherwise might not get. People interested in helping in this way should channel their giving through a reputable organization so that their efforts reach the children they want to help.

But despite the efforts of many humanitarian organizations around the world, thousands of orphanages have never received outside help of any kind. There simply are many, many forgotten children.

Many humanitarian organizations, including ours, have sponsorship programs linking needy but nonadoptable children with "sponsor" families. In addition to providing financially for a child, sponsorship gives the child a relationship with a family who can love him or her, though it be long-distance, who can remember special holidays and can pray for the child. These programs are strong and successful.

But long-distance parenting can't notice skinned knees, hear bedtime prayers or be sensitive to hurt feelings or loneliness.

If you live in a country that has a foster-care system for needy children, you can consider becoming a foster parent to a child who otherwise may miss the stability and love of the home you could provide. Every state in the United States is hungry for good families who are willing to provide temporary homes for children while they wait for adoptive families or for their biological families to resolve problems that temporarily rendered them unfit to have custody of their children. Or, if you live near an orphanage, you can consider volunteering time to tutor or read to or share one of your skills with a child or children who live in its confines.

Adoption: A Two-Way Solution

Still, even in the best of conditions, an institution or foster-care system can't nurture a child in the same way a family can. Adoption is a better solution for these children. Yet not all legally adoptable orphans will be adopted. Some will not survive the hardship of their conditions. Others live in countries that do not allow foreign adoptions because government officials do not understand adoption and are fearful of the consequences. Thousands of other children could be adopted except that (contrary to many people's perceptions) there simply are not enough families willing to open their hearts and homes to adopt them.

For many, adoption is seen solely as a substitute for biological children in infertile families. And it *is* a wonderful way to create a family for parents unable to produce biological children. I have welcomed family after family at the airport, witnessing the incredible joy a long-awaited child brings to a couple without hope of producing a biological child. The atmosphere at the gate is much like that of the delivery room in a hospital. In fact, it has my own children confused! One day I overheard my then five- and six-year-old arguing in the playroom and went to listen a moment unobserved behind the door before going in to arbitrate. They were at a stand-off, hands on hips, glaring at one another, and this is what I heard:

"Andrea, that's *not* where babies come from!"

Mark paused—for dramatic emphasis, I'm sure—and then continued in a much louder voice to show how strongly he felt:

"Babies come from *the airport!*"

And they do, for many special families.

A little girl recently found a new home with a family in the United States. This two-year-old moppet was found by overseas officials wandering the streets, abandoned by her family. Authorities named her Valentina, appropriate for this blond gift of love. Her adoptive mom has a physical disability which causes her some difficulty in walking and which precluded her from risking pregnancy. In her new home not even a week, Valentina began taking her new mom's hand to lead her when walking. This happy child sings all day long. Imagine the incomparable joy this family has experienced.

Another family began to pray for a baby boy to join their two girls. They had lost twin boys in childbirth, and yet had not requested or prayed for twins. Imagine their amazement when we called to ask if they would consider adopting identical twin baby boys! Adoption can bring great joy to families who have experienced loss.

But adoption brings tremendous joy to others as well. Birthing many boys made us playfully suggest to all our family and friends that we had a little boy mold, and that if we birthed ten children they would all be boys, all looking just alike. We decided not to test the theory! But bringing three children into our home through adoption, including the introduction of two little girls into our basketball team line-up, has been a thrill we didn't know we would ever experience. As a mother I have enjoyed ribbons and dresses in addition to the athletic shoes and jeans to which I had become so accustomed. Our family is richer as it has grown and changed into a multicultural, multiethnic family.

Another pastor's family birthed boys, and for years the mom had talked and dreamed of a daughter who would be named Kate. As they became aware of children overseas who needed homes they decided to adopt a girl. When a little girl was suggested to them, they immediately knew she was their daughter when they heard her name was Katya. For many weeks after Katya joined their family, she had difficult adjustments to make, including a new language to learn. In pre-adopt classes I always tell families not to adopt with the expectation that our adopted children will be grateful to us for adopting them. So imagine the family's surprise and delight when, several months after coming to her new home, Katya said, "Mommy, thank you, thank you for coming to get me from the orphanage."

Adoption brings great joy, both to the children who receive parents to love them and to the parents who have the privilege of opening their hearts and homes to a child who needs their love and nurturing.

Looking at Children Through the Eyes of Faith
May this little prayer poem (author unknown) challenge you to pray for children and to consider how else you might become involved with a forgotten child, a child who needs parents.

We pray for children
   who put chocolate fingers everywhere,
   who like to be tickled,
   who stomp in puddles and ruin their new pants,
   who sneak Popsicles before supper,
   who erase holes in math workbooks,
   who can never find their shoes.

And we pray for those
   who stare at photographers from behind barbed wire,
   who can't bound down the street in new sneakers,
   who never "counted potatoes,"
   who are born in places we wouldn't be caught dead in,
   who never go to the circus,
   who live in an X-rated world.

We pray for children
   who bring us sticky kisses and fistfuls of dandelions,

who sleep with the cat and bury goldfish,
who hug us in a hurry and forget their lunch money,
who cover themselves with Band-Aids and sing off key,
who squeeze toothpaste all over the sink,
who slurp their soup.

And we pray for those
who never get dessert,
who have no safe blanket to drag behind them,
who can't find any bread to steal,
who don't have any rooms to clean up,
whose pictures aren't on anybody's dresser,
whose monsters are real.

We pray for children
who spend all their allowance before Tuesday,
who throw tantrums in the grocery store and pick at their
food,
who like ghost stories,
who shove dirty clothes under the bed,
who get visits from the tooth fairy,
who don't like to be kissed in front of the car pool,
who squirm in church and scream on the phone,
whose tears we sometimes laugh at and whose smiles can
make us cry.

And we pray for those
whose nightmares come in the daytime,
who will eat anything,
who have never seen a dentist,
who are never spoiled by anyone,
who go to bed hungry and cry themselves to sleep,
who live and move, but have no being.

We pray for children
   who want to be carried
   and for those who must,
   for those we never give up on
   and for those who never get a second chance,
   for those we smother . . .
   and for those who will grab the hand of anybody kind
   enough to offer it.

We pray for children. Amen

3

IS ADOPTION
SECOND-BEST?

Which of you, if his son asks for bread, will give
him a stone? Or if he asks for a fish, will give
him a snake? If you, then, though you are evil,
know how to give good gifts to your children,
how much more will your Father in heaven give
good gifts to those who ask him! So in everything,
do to others what you would have them do to you.
MATTHEW 7:9-12

D O YOU STRUGGLE WITH THE IDEA OF ADOPTION AS A WAY TO create a family? Then this chapter is for you. Some husbands are dragging their feet because they desire an heir by blood. Some women feel they must savor the kicks of a baby within them in order to experience true motherhood. Other people look to adoption because they have experienced disappointment in their lives, either failing to become married, or losing a child, or missing the privilege of birthing children of both genders. You may want to adopt, but fears lurk in your mind and you wonder if you will be doing the right thing. You may fear the timing, the unknowns, the choice of a child. In all of these situations, only you can decide if adoption is right for you. This chapter will address those lingering doubts and fears regarding the choice to adopt and I hope, lay them to rest by putting it all in perspective.

Making Peace with the Past

First of all, everyone considering adoption needs to make peace with his or her past. If there are unresolved issues in your life or in the life of your spouse, it is important to resolve them before entering into the new relationships created by adoption. Once a new child or children enter into your home, personal issues are compounded because there are more people who are affected by them. A child will also bring into your family relationship personal issues that will demand your attention. He or she deserves to have parents who are anchored and ready to devote time to the child's needs instead their own. It is essential to ask ourselves the questions "What has brought me to this place of considering adoption?" and "What is my motivation?"

Each person reading this book will have a different response to these questions. For a couple to successfully parent an adopted child, they need to be united in their decision to adopt, but they may have different motivations.

Motivations Can Differ

For some couples, it is disappointing to realize that they have different motivations for adoption. Ron and I were such a couple. There is no question that, of the two of us, it is I who feel more passion regarding orphan children and adoption. After all, I am the one who is an adopted child myself. I cannot even explain the depth of emotion and love I feel for little children around the world who are unable to grow up with the love and nurture of adoring parents. I feel called to be a voice for these innocent children whom I know are also very close to God's heart.

I also love being a mother and love the privilege of parenting a large family. On his own, without the input I bring to our relationship, Ron would probably not have pursued adoption. After birthing our four sons, Ron would have been content to consider our family complete. But after talking and praying together, we realized that I had both a passion to share our home with a needy child and a desire to have the experience of mothering a little girl. Neither of us was looking for a project. In a joint decision we decided to pursue adoption.

Did Ron suddenly develop a passion for additional children or an insatiable desire to be daddy to a little girl? Not to the degree that I did. We were united in our desire to adopt, but we were initially prompted by different motives. I wanted to open my heart and home to another child to love. Ron's motive was a desire to show his love to me by giving me the desire of my heart—an adopted child. I have explained our choice of adoption to people through the years in this way. Some husbands give their wives the gift of a Caribbean cruise or diamond earrings. Mine gives me the gift of adopting children. And I adore him for it.

Did an initial difference in motivation mean Ron does not share in parenting our adopted children? Does it mean that because I was the initiator in adoption, our adopted children are my responsibility, and when challenges arise with those children it is my fault because I wanted them and he did not? No.

We originally approached our decision to adopt from different perspectives—but we were united in our decision to adopt. We both realized that our decision to adopt had to go far beyond our initial reasons for looking into adoption. A decision to adopt cannot be based on a desire to be humanitarian or to fulfill a void in our own lives or even to please a husband or wife—it must be based on a desire to love a child without any expectation from him or her in return. This is an important distinction. In order to have a successful parenting experience, a couple needs to be united in their decision to adopt, and that decision must be based on a desire to love a child, even if they initially have different motivations. This unity of decision and the desire to give love to a child is the glue that binds a couple together in their adoption journey.

Making Peace with Your Past

For many who choose to adopt, the motivation is infertility. And adoption is a wonderful way to create a family for people in this situation. But if you feel that adoption is a disappointing second-best alternative to biological parenting, it is important to resolve these feelings before an adopted child joins your family.

There is great pain when a couple who longs for a child receives the news that they will never biologically produce the child they ache for. Perhaps you know of a husband who longs to share the sport he excels in with a little boy who looks like him. Having a son to carry on the family name, passed on from generations before, may be a bitterly shattered dream for you or for someone you know. For the wife who has taken her temperature day in and day out and so looked forward to pregnancy that she even has maternity clothes hanging in her closet, the pain of loss may be almost unbearable.

You may be grieving over the inability to bear children, still carrying the pain and anger of that disappointment, when an adopted child comes into your home. Or you may have lost a child to accident or illness and still be feeling anger and grief when you adopt a son or daughter to fill the empty space. If you have experienced the death of a child, you have known an excruciating pain that is unmatched by any other and that will never totally go away. You need to clearly grasp that your adopted child will not replace the child you lost; he or she is a new and separate gift to you.

Maybe you are a single woman who has had a great desire to be married and have a family, yet as the years have unfolded that dream simply has never materialized. Adoption can be a happy way for many single women to experience the joys of parenthood and to give a new life to a child who longs for a home. But once again it is important for a single woman to make peace with her singleness before pursuing adoptive motherhood. If you are bitter toward life or marriage, men or God, and these feelings are not resolved before you become a mother, you will model these angry feelings to your little child.

In like manner, if a biological parent is angry at having failed to produce the boy or girl of which he or she dreamed, those angry feelings, if not resolved, will eventually be communicated to his or her children, perhaps hurting them irreparably. Think what damage it could do to a little boy, for instance, if his perception was "What she really wants is a daughter, not a son."

Children feel their parents' emotions. Deal with and talk about your anger and disappointment. Otherwise the adopted child will perhaps even feel responsible for your hurt and will feel he or she is second-best. For a successful parenting relationship, parents need to make peace with their past.

Allowing God to Be God

We can help ourselves make peace with the past by allowing God to be God in our lives and in our circumstances. What do I mean by this statement? The thought may even seem elementary to you. You may be thinking, "Of course God is God!" But if you're anything like me, it is often easier to say that God is God than to allow that reality to penetrate your life. Let me show you what I mean.

I married my college sweetheart, Paul, and we had a story-book wedding and honeymoon. Four months later we discovered that my new husband had inoperable cancer. The ink on our thank-you notes was barely dry, and the family we giggled about starting was only a distant dream, when suddenly our lives and future were on hold. Candlelight dinners, newly unpacked wedding presents and dreamy nighttime talks about our future were replaced by hours spent in hospital corridors with medicinal smells, countless lab tests and grave talks with physicians who did not dare to predict our future. Two years after our wedding, the memories still painfully fresh in our minds, Paul died.

During his illness, I had focused on Scriptures concerning healing, choosing a promise in Matthew 21:22 which read, "If you believe, you will receive anything you ask for in prayer." I had clung fiercely to that verse, believing that if I had enough trust, God would certainly answer my prayer and completely heal Paul. I wanted my strong, athletic husband healed more than anything else in the world. I believed with my whole heart that God would surely honor the promise in this verse because I had total trust that he was capable of performing miracles. But taking this verse out of context, and excluding other essential principles in Scripture, I put the entire burden of responsibility for Paul's healing on myself instead of on God. I thought that if I believed hard enough, Paul would be healed.

But that kind of faulty thinking put me in charge of the future instead of God. I was willing to trust God—as long as he was willing to answer my prayer in the way that I wanted. But I was not willing to trust God with a different outcome. In fact, I was not willing to allow God to be God! I wanted to dictate to him how the events in my life should unfold, and I would not entertain the thought of anything else. The dreams of marriage and family I had visualized throughout my life had nearly been penciled in on my schedule book, and pictures of our first home and future children were real, complete with names, colors, sounds and smells, in my mind. I felt that I knew what was best for me and anything else was unacceptable. Some of you who have faced the reality of infertility blocking your dream of a family may identify with my feelings. Others will identify for separate reasons.

I felt a tremendous burden of responsibility by choosing to be in charge of my life. In trusting my own plans for the future, my plans for a life and ministry with Paul, I was essentially telling God that I did not and could not trust him to take care of me. I had believed in God from my earliest memories as a child, but now, facing a tremendously difficult time in my life, I realized that I was not allowing him to be God in my life. I did not love and trust him enough to let him be in charge of my future. I did not love him enough to allow him to say no to my request. I was not convinced that he loved me enough to take better care of me than I could take of myself.

Countless people like me dream dreams we pray will become reality. We pray for a marriage partner. We dream of pregnancy. We pray for a son—or a daughter. Perhaps we dream of twins. In our hopes for our lives, infertility does not exist. Nor does singleness or sickness or delayed fulfillment of any of our dreams. But when our hopes do not become reality and our lives do not progress according to our plans, many people have trouble allowing God to be God in their lives, just as I did.

Blaming God

Many of us blame God for our disappointments, for our childlessness or failure to be married. Some of us may respond to our heartaches the way one of my sons did when he was very little. I can still recall being upstairs putting our baby in bed for his mid-morning nap when I heard a heart-thumping crash downstairs.

Facing the dilemma of not wanting to awaken the baby by yelling out or by bolting out of his room, I forced myself to listen for several seconds, straining to assess the circumstances. What I heard next were a piercing scream and then loud footsteps stomping down the hallway, turning and beginning to climb the stairs. Hurriedly placing the baby in his crib in hopes of reaching the nursery door before the angry stomper reached it himself, I emerged from the nursery with one hand behind me, willing the door not to squeak.

I met my furious two-year-old at the top of the stairs, his eyebrows locked in disgust. His lip was puffy and bleeding. Just by looking at him I could tell what had happened. It seems he had been running a lap around our kitchen, dining room, living room, entry and family room, knowing I was upstairs and would not likely catch him in this forbidden yet overwhelmingly tempting activity. In the reckless abandon he felt in his secret adventure, he tripped on the stair between the sunken family room and the kitchen, gashing his lip on the metal edge of the stair. His smoldering eyes revealed that he was more angry than hurt. When they met mine, he shook his fist menacingly at me, snarling, "Mommy, I hurt myself because *you* weren't there to watch out for me!"

In a similar way, we shake our fists at God and blame him for the hurts in our lives. I'm not talking about the things that are our own fault, like my toddler's carelessness in running through the house and then tripping because of his own foolish behavior. I'm thinking about circumstances in our lives that cause us great pain and yet are completely out of our control, like infertility, or miscarriage, or a child claimed by meningitis, or an accidental drowning.

Is it God's fault when things like these go wrong? I can still relive the conversation I had with an acquaintance just days after Paul died of cancer. She admonished, "Praise God for Paul's death!" I wanted to punch her. Although I know theologies differ on the subject, I felt angry because I did not think God *wanted* Paul to die so soon after his college graduation and our marriage. I felt cheated of our life together. I certainly was not going to praise God for something which caused me such anguish.

Nor do I believe that God wants infertility or miscarriages or any of the other hurts and harmful things that happen in the world. Both good and evil are present in the world. But whether or not we believe that God *causes* the hurt in the world, we cannot deny that he *allows* these things to occur. We know from Scripture that God is sovereign, that he is in control of the world and therefore could prevent the hurtful and bad from occurring.

Yet sometimes he allows pain and suffering in our lives. However, being God, he can take those hurtful and even evil things and turn them into good in our lives. He promises us, in Romans 8:28, "All things work together for good to those who . . . are called according to his purpose." God is the only one who can take our disappointments and turn them into good. He is the only one who can pierce the future to foresee the way our hurts and disappointments will resolve. This ability to see ahead is what I call an eternal perspective. Perhaps you are shaking your fist at God for a disappointment in your life. How can you or I move from this place of blaming God for our past, for the circumstances in our lives, to trusting that he loves us and wants the best for us? How can we allow God to be God in our lives?

Cultivating an Eternal Perspective

For me, the exercise of cultivating an eternal perspective helps me as I seek to allow God to be God in my life. What is an eternal perspective? I see only a very small portion of my life. In contrast, God sees our circumstances with the big picture in mind. Cultivating an eternal perspective is the exercise of trying to look at the events in our lives in the way that God may look at them, realizing that he will use everything, both good and bad, together for good.

I will never forget the year Tad, age twelve, had a tonsillectomy. For months he had struggled with on-again off-again tonsillitis and antibiotics in an alternating pattern. Finally we succumbed to the decision of elective surgery. While the surgery was successful, recovery was very painful, and our usually active, good-natured son missed two weeks of school because of his weak and listless condition.

Valentine's Day approached, and our four boys decided to silk-screen valentines for all their classmates. (As a former art teacher I sometimes feel guilty that I don't do more art projects at home with my own children, but I must admit I don't like the mess!) So I helped each of the boys design and cut paper stencils and assembled our materials, including jars of thick, bright magenta, yellow and blue printing ink. We soon had freshly screened valentines drying all over the floors of several rooms, each screened three times to get full-color printing.

After the last ink splotches were cleaned from the floor and the dried valentines were stacked, signed and ready for school, Tad asked if he could write notes on his valentines. He had participated only as an observer in the project, traveling back and forth between the kitchen print shop and his "bed" on the family-room couch. He propped himself on a elbow on his couch and painstakingly spent hours writing greetings to his friends. He would not go to bed until he had written notes to every one of his classmates. The last thing he said before he went to bed was, "Don't forget to bring my valentines home tomorrow!"

When I went to school the next day, instead of the usual bulging bag of valentines, there were only two envelopes addressed to my son. Knowing he would be devastated, I stopped at the store and bought some candies and valentine treats, hoping to diffuse the hurt. But as soon as I walked in the front door, Tad called out, "I'm in here, Mom. Bring my valentines in here!" I tried to focus his attention on the snacks I had brought, but my son's only interest was in the valentines he had been thinking all day about receiving. When the realization that he had only received two valentines began to penetrate, he began to cry, feeling forgotten and lonely.

That evening was very long and quiet, far different from the festive atmosphere we had experienced the night before in our preparation for Valentine's Day. All of us felt very sad until the phone rang. My husband answered. The caller was one of the teachers from our children's school, calling about an unrelated matter. Before ending the conversation, Ron asked if the teacher knew anything about the sixth-grade Valentine's party. "Oh, yes," he said, "Didn't you hear? The sixth graders decided to use their Valentine money for underprivileged kids instead of exchanging valentines and having a party."

Suddenly our whole perspective changed. Seconds before, we were devastated to think that our son had been so overlooked. Now, as we understood the whole picture, it became a delightful compliment to our son that he had been so highly thought of that he had received two valentines!

This is what I mean when I talk about cultivating an eternal perspective. Our vision is very limited compared to what God sees. Sometimes the very circumstance that seems so very devastating, like a failed *in vitro* attempt or an adoption that falls through—and that certainly feels like second-best from our vantage point—can eventually be viewed as a blessing as we see it in a larger context.

Just as we can see only our immediate circumstances, sometimes we see only immediate disappointment in our circumstances and miss out on the bigger picture of what God may have in store for us. Although it is hard to look past whatever it is that has caused us pain, as we allow ourselves to realize that God sees a bigger picture than we do, perhaps we can trust him, knowing that he is the only one who can cause good to come out of tragedy.

On a Sunday afternoon many years ago, an unmarried young woman faced life-threatening emergency surgery for ovarian tumors. She survived the surgery but was left with the uncomfortable effects of menopause in her very early twenties and the devastating knowledge that she would never bear children. Her immediate circumstances had to leave her discouraged, wondering if she would ever become a wife or experience the joy of motherhood. No one could say these circumstances were good ones!

But many years later, looking at her situation through the perspective of eternity, the very circumstance which was the hardest for her to face, her infertility, has become a blessing in her life. That woman is my mother, and though unrelated biologically because I am adopted, we are as close friends as any mother and daughter can be. We are very grateful to God for bringing us into each other's lives. I attribute the passion I feel for orphan children and the adoption work I do around the world today to my mother. If she had not experienced the pain of infertility in her young life, we would not have experienced the joy of which I am one of the recipients.

Charles Swindoll recounts the true story of a Norwegian fisherman who left in the morning with his two sons on their daily fishing expedition. By the middle of the afternoon the waves began to rise and pitch the boat back and forth in the biting, salty wind. As the three of them rowed desperately to reach the shore before the storm unleashed its full fury, the light in the lighthouse suddenly went dead, leaving them with no guidance to reach the shore.

At the same time, at home in their cottage, the wife was trying to fix dinner in anticipation of her family's return. A fire broke out in the kitchen, spreading quickly and uncontrollably throughout the house, destroying everything. The wife escaped with only the clothes she was wearing. She waited tearfully on the shore to tell her husband and sons the terrible news.

"Karl, we lost our house and everything we have in a fire," the wife began when the men came ashore, but Karl didn't seem moved by her upsetting news. She wondered if he had not heard because of the deafening noise of the pounding waves, and so she tried again. "Karl, we lost everything!" she cried.

This time he responded, "I heard you, Ingrid. But a few hours ago we were out in the storm at sea, rowing as hard as we were able, wondering if we would ever make it to the shore. When the lighthouse went dead we didn't even know where the shore was. And then, suddenly, we began to see a yellow glow in the distance which grew bigger and bigger. Finally we could see the shoreline and we rowed safely here. You see, Ingrid, that yellow glow was the first sight of our house on fire. At the peak of the blaze we could see the shoreline as bright as day. The same fire that destroyed our house created the light that saved our lives."

Often we see only our own present circumstances, but God sees beyond them to a bigger picture. If we realize that God sees a panoramic view and can work both the good and the bad together for our good, it can cause us to relax and to rejoice. Those circumstances that seem to be second-best may not be second-best at all!

Biblical Examples of Adoption

God is concerned about our difficult circumstances. He established the family as his primary means of taking care of children; he also grieves when children must be without parents.

There are several illustrations in the Bible that show God using adoption to provide for children without parents. Let's look at two of them. Moses was one such child. When the declaration went forth in Egypt that all Hebrew baby boys must be killed, Moses' mother hid him. After three months in hiding she realized she could no longer protect him, so she prepared a waterproof basket and set her baby in the Nile River.

As is the case with most birth mothers who abandon their babies, this mother did not let him go because she did not love him, but because she felt she had no other choice. She wanted her baby to be found so that another could provide the care she was unable to give. And so it came to be that the abandoned Moses was found; the adoptive mother who raised him was the Egyptian daughter of Pharaoh. God used adoption to save Moses' life and to provide a qualified leader to lead Israel out of Egypt.

Esther is another biblical example of an adopted child. Her story, found in Esther 2, relates that she was an orphan girl raised by her cousin Mordecai. When the decree went out announcing a contest to replace the deposed queen Vashti of Persia, Mordecai realized that Esther, who was very beautiful, might be chosen. He counseled her carefully not to reveal her Hebrew heritage and then allowed her to participate in the beauty contest. She received great favor with the king and was declared queen. God later used Esther and her relationship with Mordecai to protect the Jewish people from death. Once again God used adoption both to protect a child's life and to accomplish his purposes.

Today, too, adoption provides a family for a child who otherwise would not have had one, as well as working out God's special purpose in that child's life and the lives of people around that child.

God Adopts Us as His Children

God uses the metaphor of adoption to explain his covenant relationship with us. When we accept his gift of salvation, he adopts us as his children; it is the same permanent parent-child relationship that an adoptive family experiences. Listen to these words in Ephesians 1:3-5 describing God's adoption of us:

> Praise be to the God and Father of our Lord Jesus Christ, who has blessed us in the heavenly realms with every spiritual blessing in Christ. For he chose us in him before the creation of the world to be holy and blameless in his sight. In love he predestined us to be adopted as his sons through Jesus Christ, in accordance with his pleasure and will—to the praise of his glorious grace, which he has freely given us in the One he loves. In him we have redemption through his blood, the forgiveness of sins, in accordance with the riches of God's grace that he lavished on us with all wisdom and understanding.

Just as adoptive parents long for the day when they will bring their adopted children home, so God yearns for the day when he will receive us as his children—when he will graft us into his family.

Families sometimes wonder if they will be able to love an adopted child as much as they would their own flesh and blood. To illustrate the intimate closeness of the relationship we enjoy with God, God chose the word *adoption*. Since God used this word to describe our relationship with him as his true children, even heirs, we have a model for adoption symbolizing an equal relationship to a biological one.

Will we love an adopted child as much as a birth child? Before adopting children I pondered the same question myself. I can say now, having both biological and adopted children, that they are *all* our children. I would give my life for any one of them. Countless families of adopted children would say the same.

When we accept God's offer of forgiveness of our sins, we are the recipients of God's grace. Adoption, too, is an outpouring of God's grace on all of the persons involved. Birth parents are recipients of a loving home for the child for whom they are not able to care. Adopted children are recipients of parents to love them and tell them they are special. Adoptive parents are recipients of a child to love and nurture. Looking at the Bible shows us that adoption is an incredible outpouring of God's love, a topic about which he cares very much. That God could accomplish such joy out of the tragedy of a child without parents is a miracle of grace. Adoption is clearly God's design.

Blessing from Pain

Another tool that can help us make peace with unresolved issues in our lives is the realization that God can use our circumstances, both good and bad, to build character and give us blessings. A woman tells her story of living in Pakistan many years ago with her husband and family when her six-month-old baby died.

An old man who heard of their grief came to comfort them. He explained, "A tragedy like this is similar to being plunged into boiling water. If you are an egg, your affliction will make you hard-boiled and unresponsive. It you are a potato, you will emerge soft and pliable, resilient and adaptable."

The woman declared, "It may sound funny to God, but there have been many times since that day when I have prayed, 'Lord, let me be a potato.'"[1]

Miscarriages, infertility, singleness, longing for a son or a daughter, losing a son or daughter, feeling pushed into parenting by a spouse—all of these life situations are like being plunged into boiling water. Any one of them can make us bitter and hard people, feeling life has treated us unfairly. It would not be surprising for someone to respond in this way.

But we can choose to respond in another way—we can allow these circumstances to make us resilient and adaptable. Maybe we won't ever experience a baby kicking within us, but that doesn't mean we can't be a mother in every sense of the word to a young child who needs a mother and might not otherwise live. Maybe we didn't birth the biological son or daughter we longed to produce, but if we can look beyond the hurt, we can still provide a home for a little girl or boy who needs a parent to give love and say, "You're special." Instead of focusing on bitterness, we have the amazing privilege of providing a home for a child who otherwise might not have any chance in life at all.

God can take our disappointments and fears and turn them into good if we give him that chance. Second-best? Not in God's eyes.

4

ETHICS OF ADOPTION

"Do not take advantage of a widow or an orphan.
If you do and they cry out to me,
I will certainly hear their cry."
EXODUS 22:22-23

E HAVE TALKED ABOUT HOW ADOPTION IS A WONDERFUL way for a parentless child to experience love and tender nurturing, an enriching means for adoptive parents to offer a child a home, a comfort to birth parents who want better for their children than they are able to provide. Adoption is also a caring solution for governments that realize children need more than life in an institution if they are to grow into healthy adults. Well, since adoption is so wonderful, why isn't it more widely done?

The issues surrounding adoption are often scary and overwhelming for all parties involved. In fact, it is the ethics of adoption that sometimes dissuade people from experiencing what can be a wonderful and satisfying relationship. Let's take a look and try to understand.

Buying and Selling of Children

We have all heard stories of people viewing innocent children as salable commodities. Honest, law-abiding people shrink from becoming involved in activities with questionable ethics. Yet throughout history children have been bought and sold.

Is baby-buying occurring in our world today? Yes, it is. Are all children who are adopted bought? No! But it is important to know that money, even large amounts of it, can be exchanged for children, and more important to know how this problem can be avoided.

I will never forget my experience of standing in a sugar-beet field thousands of miles from home talking to the birth parents of a four-month-old baby girl whom Ron and I were hoping to adopt. We had found Rosina languishing in a baby orphanage, abandoned at birth by parents too poor to care for her. We needed their signatures of relinquishment in order to adopt her, and we had traveled many miles over bumpy dirt roads to seek them. We were not stuck in rush-hour traffic, but our passage was impeded by gaggles of geese crossing the road and oxen being taken to the fields to plow. We passed by picturesque cottages adorned with colorful stenciled designs and saw children peeking curiously at the forty-year-old taxi transporting us.

The whole village of gypsies surrounded us, all watching as the fate of Rosina was discussed. Through our interpreter, Rosina's mother, Linca, challenged us, declaring that she wanted four thousand U.S. dollars for Rosina! We tried to explain to her that we hadn't come to buy Rosina, but that we would love her and give her a good home. Linca wasn't convinced. "Two thousand dollars and a car!" she countered. We did not see Linca's second offer as a come-down in price. She was a serious bargainer. We tried again to explain that we weren't there to buy her baby, but that we could educate Rosina and help her to become whatever she wanted to be. Linca retorted by dramatically throwing her hands into the air and declaring, "That's fine for my daughter, but what is there for me? Make me an offer, then."

As Ron and I talked, still standing between the mounded dirt rows in that field, farmed by hand as it had been for centuries, still surrounded by the entire village who were pressing in against us, we recognized that this village had no electricity or indoor plumbing and the houses, though quaint on the outside, were single rooms with only dirt floors on the inside. We decided to give the family a gift of $500, not as a payment for Rosina, but simply because we knew the family was very poor and could use our help. When our desire was communicated with Linca, her face brightened, and nodding she said, "It is decided: Rosina will go to the United States." Her response showed us she did not understand. In her mind, she had just sold her daughter for $500. We wondered how we could make her understand that we were giving her a gift, not a price.

The next day at the courthouse, the attorney who was to draw up the papers for our adoption explained that it was not legal to give the birth parents anything, even a gift, in order to adopt their child. But he also explained to us that many people choose to break this law, and that the decision was up to us. Knowing how much a little girl meant to me, Ron deferred the decision to me. We tried to explain to Linca that we wanted to adopt her baby, but since it was not legal, we would not be able to give her the money. She responded by vigorously shaking her head from side to side, a gesture which needed no language interpretation. The communication was very clear: no money, no baby!

I can still smell the stale smell of smoke in that courthouse packed with people where I made one of the most difficult decisions of my life. I wanted to adopt a little girl. But as the tears escaped down my cheeks in that anything-but-private courthouse—as people watched us and even pointed their fingers at my display of emotion—I knew that I wanted to honor Christ even more than I wanted to adopt a little girl. We did not choose to go through with the adoption of Rosina.

There are many other cases of birth families in all countries of the world wanting money or goods in exchange for the adoption of their children. Across the ocean in another country, as our car stopped temporarily in a tiny village, a young woman came up to the car window holding her baby out to me. I smiled at her, thinking she wanted me to admire her sweet baby. Then she raised up seven fingers signaling her price for that baby.

This problem is occurring in the U.S. too. We are aware of young women who will come to more than one adoption agency to discuss placing their babies with adoptive families. Then they may promise their baby to families in several agencies, receiving money from each for housing, food and pregnancy-related expenses. Once a birth mother said to me, "I know I can get whatever I want from a family, because I'm giving them the most valuable gift they'll ever receive."

Although it is easy to pass judgment on women like Linca and these others in the world who make decisions to sell or profit financially from their children, most of us have never lived in circumstances that prompted such decisions. Although we know it certainly is not right to sell a child, perhaps we can feel compassion on those who live in the kind of conditions where they feel pressured to sell their own flesh and blood.

Baby Brokers

But it is not only birth families who can be involved in this unethical process. There are baby brokers who realize that they can profit financially from adoption. They are the middle people who bring the desired "product," the child, to the "customer," the adoption agency or adoptive parent. These people may buy or steal babies and then turn around and sell them to agencies or adoptive families. I have heard heart-breaking stories of children stolen from maternity hospitals or even from the arms of unsuspecting mothers and then black-marketed. This practice, too, has happened in every country in the world, including our own. These brokers prey on the innocent—the children, the birth parents and the adoptive families.

However, if people did not buy, there would be no sales. One day our adoption agency received a call from a pleasant-sounding woman who unashamedly offered $50,000 for a healthy child. She had such a longing to be a mother that she was willing to become one at any cost. And she is not an isolated incident. There are others willing to pay from a different motivation. Child pornography and child prostitution rings have invaded developing countries to buy innocent children, transporting them into lives of horror.

Valid Adoption Costs

Knowing that baby selling and buying exists, how does a family who is moved toward the plight of parentless children reconcile the costs of adoption? Even for people who find the selling of babies abhorrent, still there are costs. How can this be? One day a woman called into our office and explained that they and several families they knew wanted to adopt children from overseas. When we explained the programs available and the costs involved, the woman became irate, arguing, "You should be paying us to adopt these children! We are doing you and the babies a favor!"

I understand her line of reasoning, and there are many, many people who agree with her. With good coverage a fam-

ily can birth a baby for little cost beyond insurance. Yet adopting a baby is expensive. Expensive even without unethical
and under-the-table practices!

There are many justified expenses related to facilitating an
adoption. Orphans Overseas, for example, has low overhead
because our offices are donated to us rent-free. In addition,
many of our staff volunteer their time, an unselfish gift,
because they have a passion for needy children. Still our costs
are significant. Although we don't pay bribes, we do pay our
overseas staff reasonable wages for their work. Many papers
are needed and many levels of government must give their
consent to an adoption; there are costs related to each of these
steps. Communication and staff travel costs add to the
expense. In addition, a good percentage of our revenue goes
back into the country to fund care programs for the nonadoptable orphans.

Even in a domestic adoption there is significant valid
expense. In the U.S., most birth mothers will choose to receive
medical care through an obstetrician and deliver their babies
in the hospital. Some of these young women will have insurance coverage, but others will not. Some of the young women
will be recipients of state-funded medical welfare during pregnancy; some will not. The adoptive family often agrees to
cover unpaid medical expenses. Reasonable expenses for
maternity clothes, prenatal vitamins, living expenses during
pregnancy and time lost from work are also valid expenses.
Expensive gifts, cars, vacations and college educations are not.

Even though the costs related to adoption may feel like paying for a child, an adoptive family can feel at peace regarding
costs once they understand which expenses are justified.

Choosing a Child
Another ethical question with which adoptive families must

grapple is "How do you choose a child?" With biological children there is no ethical issue at all—we get whatever comes. But this issue is a concern in adoption. Who matches children and families? If there is a limited number of adoptive families available, who decides which children receive families and which do not? Or in the reverse situation, if the number of adoptable babies is limited, who decides which families become parents and which do not? To many of us looking at these questions it feels as if someone is placed in the position of "playing God."

I vividly remember being led up and down row after row of rusting, peeling cribs in an orphanage, viewing children. When we completed our tour, the director politely asked me through an interpreter, "Which child would you like?"

I can still feel the wave of sickness that washed over me in that moment as I thought, *This isn't right! I can't choose a child like I choose a loaf of bread in the grocery store!* I responded, "Which child is available for adoption?"

I couldn't justify selecting a child's future just as I would select a puppy from a newborn litter. I know myself. I am drawn either to the puppy I think is cutest or to the forlorn runt of the litter because I feel sorry for it. Neither one was a good method for choosing the future destiny of a child, who is infinitely more valuable than a puppy. I felt an overwhelming sadness for the ones I couldn't choose. I was totally unable to make a selection, and so we left the orphanage.

In a similar fashion, sometimes families are able to select children from photographs and videos. Occasionally we have pictures available for our adoptive families. But what kind of criteria do a family use in selecting an heir and permanent family member? I am not suggesting that it is wrong to have a desire to see the physical characteristics of a child. But there is much more to be considered than a child's physical looks.

I will never know, but I might not have selected my birth children from a hospital nursery if I had compared them to the other babies born that same day and had based my decision on looks alone. Yet I can't imagine having missed out on the joy I have experienced with each of these beautiful children.

How will you go about choosing the age, gender, nationality and race of your adopted child? Is it better to match as closely to your biological roots as is possible? In the early history of adoption in the United States, social workers worked very hard to match every aspect of a family's background with that of an adopted child. Nationality, hair and eye color, interests, educational background and religion were some of the considerations. Part of the reasoning behind such painstaking care was the belief that it was better if it was not widely known that the child was adopted.

Unless someone studies eye color in my immediate and extended family and realizes I possess the only brown eyes in a totally blue-eyed crowd, no one would ever guess that I am adopted. My Scandinavian background and blond hair fit into my adopted family because it was all carefully matched. But as the passing of years gives more understanding to adoption, social workers realize it is not a stigma needing to be hidden. Successful adoptions can occur with all kinds of matches, regardless of ethnicity or background.

Value of Children

When my son Luke goes out into the field behind our house to bring his four horses into the barn for the night, they come in a definite order that never varies. Snoopy, a bay-colored Arabian mare, always comes first, followed by Broadway, a yearling, then Caprice, Snoopy's filly, and finally Onnie, Broadway's Arabian gray mom, is always last.

There seems to be a "pecking order" in adopted children as

well. Several colleagues and I, discussing our lists of waiting families, noted that over 80 percent of our families want girls. And these statistics seem to be mirrored nationwide. Are girls more valuable? If so, the United States is probably the only country in the world who thinks so! Some people may see girls as more compliant and easier to raise. Others have a concern for the girl babies who are rejected or thrown away in some parts of the world.

We have noticed that most often it is the woman who is the initiator in adoption; the man may be less eager or may even drag his feet. Most often the women seem to desire girls. Men seem to struggle more with a desire to have a biological son rather than an adopted son as an heir. Perhaps as men grow more comfortable with adoption, these statistics will change.

Are children of one race more highly valued than those of another? When we consider opening our home to love a forgotten child we must examine our own values and ethics. Can we open our hearts to a child of a different ethnic background or race, realizing we thereby change forever into a multiethnic, multiracial family? For some families, this is a difficult question to consider. For others it is natural. Relatives may have strong feelings about this matter too.

One family who was considering overseas adoption came back to us very disappointed, complaining that their family emphatically declared, "No commies!" The prospective grandparents had vivid recollections of the fears they had experienced years before, worrying about a communist takeover of the world. They couldn't imagine having a grandchild from a country that was formerly an enemy of the United States. Though it is wise to seek extended family's blessing for an adoption, and we certainly hope for their approval, it is not necessary to seek their permission.

We have to face the fact that some families, despite our

desires, will never treat adopted family members in the same way they treat the rest of the family. I know of a family who had one adopted granddaughter and two biological grand-daughters. As the children grew up and married, the aging adoptive grandparents revised their will. They left their adopt-ed granddaughter one dollar and divided a large portion of their estate equally between their biological granddaughters. Imagine the alienation this granddaughter will feel when she learns of her grandparents' decision.

Another family suggested that an adopted grandchild should not inherit an engraved memento from his namesake grand-parent, believing that it should be given to a more distant blood relative instead. Still another family excluded the adopt-ed members from researched information about the family tree, mistakenly thinking that the adopted family members would not be interested. In this case the adopted children spoke up, declaring that family is family and that they were very much interested in their adoptive family roots! (My own children are interested in both.) However, while some families make a dis-tinction between their family members and their adoptive fam-ily members, most will treat them and love them equally.

In like manner, sometimes biological siblings in a family do not support their parents' choice to adopt. A family came to me asking what they should do in this matter. I asked the parents, "Would you ask your children's permission if you wanted to become pregnant?" They laughed at the ridiculousness of my query. Certainly, if there are already children in our home, we want their blessing. It's better if the whole family makes the decision together. But we who are parents need to remember it is ultimately our decision to make, not our children's.

Adopting with Integrity
How can we support adoption, knowing that there are some-

times questionable ethical issues involved? First of all, working with professionals who are ethical and who understand adoption well will give a prospective family a hedge of protection against unethical practices.

A family can choose among three types of adoption. They can adopt independently, through a state-licensed agency, or through a private agency. In independent adoption the adoptive family will act as their own agent, perhaps with the help of an attorney. Two of our own family's adoptions were independent adoptions, one domestic and one overseas. While these adoptions were essentially smooth ones, the overseas one would have been easier if we had worked with an agency who had been able to protect us by screening the children medically, negotiating for us, and helping us understand the pertinent adoption laws and the culture in which we were working. Some states do not allow independent adoption, and a family considering it needs to check with their own state or local regulations.

Reputable agencies can provide solid support gathered from years of experience. For example, Orphans Overseas has consistently prayed that we would be led to work with authorities who have integrity.

A government official I met on my first trip to one country said to me, "If you are who you say you are, I will allow you to do adoptions here." For several years we sponsored orphanages, trying to help make the conditions better for the orphan children who lived there. Finally I met with authorities again, this time with even higher government officials, still with hopes of receiving permission to facilitate adoptions.

I was seated at a massive ten-foot-wide table, across from the prime minister and other government officials seated in order of importance. Intimidated by the formal proceedings, I explained, "I am not here as a diplomat. I've come to speak to you as a mother and wife and as an adopted child, to speak to you from my heart about something that's very important to me, the adoption of orphan children." I went on to explain why I feel such a passion toward needy children, and I ended by asking if I could begin implementing adoptions—that day.

Then the prime minister responded to me, saying, "Now I'm going to speak to you as a father and grandfather, and I'm going to speak to you from my heart. I've heard everything you've said, and I'm going to let you start implementing adoptions—today."

In the years since then, everything these government officials said they were going to do has been done. Our prayer for integrity has been answered in our relationship with these people. Our overseas staff people treat our money as if it were their own. If they have extra after an adoption is complete, they give it back to the organization. These people share our passion for helping parentless children in an honest, ethical way. Finding an agency with whom you feel confident is important.

Agencies can be private or state-run. Private agencies may be licensed to facilitate domestic or international adoptions or both. Laws vary from state to state as to whether it is legal for an adoption agency to be a for-profit business. Costs vary greatly among private agencies. State adoption agencies focus on domestic adoptions, many of which are situations where the state has terminated the rights of the parents because of neglect or abuse. State placements are very low in costs.

It is also important to understand and adhere to international adoption laws. If I had been aware of them I could have saved myself the heartache I experienced over the gypsy baby Rosina. She had two parents who had not relinquished her and who wanted to realize financial gain through her. I did not understand the legal definition of an orphan. An orphan either has *no parents,* having lost them by death (verified by death certificates from both mother and father), abandonment, desertion or termination of parental rights, or has *one parent* who is unable to care for him or her.

Many families from the U.S. have adopted children overseas who did not legally qualify as orphans because money was paid to the birth parents, or because the child had two living parents or a single parent who had never abandoned that child. Finding a child living in filthy conditions with only a dirt floor, the eleventh or twelfth child in a family, does not in itself qualify that child for adoption. We may cry out against the poverty and sad conditions some children face. But poverty alone is not grounds for adoption. Families that adopt a child who is not legally an orphan will be unable to bring their child home. A family will avoid unethical adoption activities if they choose to work with professionals who understand and respect adoption laws, both in the U.S. and in other countries.

It Can Happen!

Most important, a family will avoid unethical adoption practices if they seek to honor Christ in all decisions regarding adoption. We know of a beautiful little baby who was being groomed to be sold for $25-30,000 U.S. from an orphanage in a developing country. She was, at two months old, the youngest baby in the orphanage. She was healthy and beautiful with half-inch-long eyelashes.

I remember very clearly the first time I saw her. She was in a room set apart from the rest of the babies in the orphanage. "Would you like this baby?" my interpreter queried. My response was immediate, "Of course I would love this baby, but how do you think we will get her without money?"

The interpreter explained that the orphanage director had recognized him from many years before as the preacher in an underground church service she had attended with her mother. When she had seen us in the orphanage, she demanded to know what we were doing there. My interpreter explained to her that he was helping me find a baby girl to adopt. "Is she a believer?" she had inquired. "Yes," he replied. "Then I will help you find a baby for no money," she promised. She had further explained to my friend that although babies were being sold to European and American couples, she did not think this practice was right, and so she would help us. She told us that if she gave us the baby's birth certificate, the baby could not be sold.

I held the baby for almost an hour, realizing that she might someday be my daughter or that (more likely) I might never see her again in my life. I held her close and crooned, "Would you like to come to Portland and have five brothers?" Her lips moved slightly. Though I knew by logic that she had no idea what I had said, I was smitten with this blue-eyed, curly-dark-haired beauty. Though I worried that she might still be sold or that someone could exchange another baby for her, six weeks later Ron returned to pick up Andrea, our first daughter.

I did not want to choose a baby. I did not want to break the law or be involved in any unethical practice regarding adoption. I wanted God to choose a child for me. And that is the way it finally happened. We feel it was meant to be. Our reunion at the airport, complete with dozens of pink helium balloons and a circle of friends, was a celebration of God's grace to us and to an innocent baby who needed a family.

5

OPEN VERSUS CLOSED ADOPTION

Administer true justice; show mercy and compassion
to one another. Do not oppress the widow or
the fatherless, the alien or the poor. In your hearts
do not think evil of each other.
ZECHARIAH 7:9-10

MANY PEOPLE WORLDWIDE RECEIVED AN UGLY INTRODUCTION to the conflicts that can erupt between birth parents and adoptive parents by witnessing the much publicized case of Baby Jessica, the little girl in the U.S. torn by a brutal tug-of-war between her biological and adoptive parents. Some people do not want to adopt because they fear that they too will encounter birth parents changing their minds and trying to take their children back. This fear of birth parents interfering in and disrupting the adoptive family's life is probably the single most feared aspect of adoption. Perhaps you fear this relationship as well.

If we explore the unique relationship that exists between birth families and adoptive families by looking at open versus closed adoptions, many of those fears should subside. You have probably heard the terms *open, closed* and *semi-open adoption*, and you may wonder what they mean.

Closed Adoption

My own adoption was a closed one. My parents went to an adoption agency, completed the necessary paperwork and home study, and waited until the agency called to tell them I was born. The social worker delivered me to my parents' home when I was five days old. She gave them verbal background information about my family but no identifying information or medical history. The agency made the placement without any input from my birth mother other than her request that I be placed in a Protestant family. My adoption records are sealed by court order; even today, if I need a birth certificate, the state must look in a special file for adopted persons. In a closed adoption, no identifying information is given to either the birth parents or the adoptive parents by the placing agency or attorney. A closed adoption is designed to protect the anonymity of both parties and to prevent any relationship between them.

Open Adoption

In contrast, an open adoption is one in which there is full disclosure of identifying information regarding both the adoptive parents and the birth parents, including names, addresses and phone numbers, and often shared aspects of parenting. Usually the birth mother has chosen the family to whom she will delegate the task of parenting her baby. Often they have spent time in each other's homes prior to the birth, and they usually share in the birth of the baby together. Sometimes the adoptive mother is the birth mother's coach in labor. Often the adoptive father cuts the umbilical cord. After the birth, the birth parent or parents will continue an ongoing relationship with the family, perhaps sharing birthdays and holidays together. The child will grow up knowing both the birth mother and the adoptive mother. An open adoption is designed to promote interaction between the birth parent and the adoptive parent, sharing the child they mutually love.

Semi-Open Adoption

A semi-open adoption is a compromise between open and closed adoptions. Most domestic adoptions today are semi-open adoptions. When a birth mother comes to us desiring to choose adoption as her parenting plan, she will most likely want to have an element of choice in the family who will parent her baby. She may tell us that she wants her child to be the first child in a family or that she does not want her child in a home with more than two children. Sometimes she wants her child to be placed out of state. Sometimes she wants to make sure her child is placed in the same city in which she lives. She will look at appropriate files designed by prospective adoptive families. These files will contain a letter which the family has written to a birth mother describing their lifestyle and goals for their children and their marriage. Identifying information is usually limited to first names and the city in which the family resides. The family will also submit a picture profile with photos of them, their home, the baby's room, and some of the activities they enjoy.

In our agency, for example, when a birth mother selects one or two families in whom she is interested, we encourage her to meet with them on a first-name-only basis. The meetings are mediated by one of our staff people and are meant to give the birth mother confidence that she is entrusting her baby to a family with whom she feels totally comfortable. Sometimes she has special considerations that are important to her. One of our birth mothers wanted the birth grandparents to be the baby's godparents. One set of birth grandparents offered to baby-sit when the adoptive mother returned to work so she would not need to use child care. Sometimes a birth mother requests a video of her baby. Sometimes the birth mother wants the adoptive parents she selects to be a part of the birth experience. Other birth mothers want the time in the hospital to be a private time for her and those closest to her to both welcome the baby and say goodby.

After the baby is born and the adoption papers are signed, in a semi-open adoption the families usually have ongoing contact through pictures and letters, but usually not personal contact. Future contacts between birth mother and adoptive parents are often mediated in a semi-open adoption or are spelled out clearly in a contract between the families. If pictures or letters are exchanged between the families, usually they will be sent to the agency or facilitating attorney's office rather than directly to each other. If one party wishes to speak to the other, again the mediator often makes the arrangements. Although to some the idea of a neutral mediator seems cumbersome, for others it provides the safeguard of knowing they will have contact with one another only when it is mutually agreed on. The birth mother usually requests pictures at birth, three months, six months, nine months, twelve months, and on Christmas and birthdays thereafter until the child turns eighteen. The agreement between birth parents and adoptive parents is usually written into a contract; the terms will vary greatly according to the birth mother's desire for contact. A semi-open adoption is designed to give birth parents some interaction with their child, yet delegates the task of parenting entirely to the adoptive family.

Advantages and Disadvantages of Closed Adoption

What are the advantages and disadvantages of closed adoption? Most overseas adoptions are closed adoptions, a fact which makes some people choose international adoption in preference to domestic adoption. People who do not want an ongoing relationship with their child's birth family may view a closed adoption as an advantage.

For families who fear that birth parents will come back to try to reclaim their children, a closed adoption may give them a feeling of more security. Financial constraints will keep most birth families in overseas countries from tracing their birth children, even if they would have the desire for additional contact. In cases where children have been abandoned, there is little chance of a birth family tracing a child placed in adoption.

Yet, although closed adoption has been the norm in international adoption until now, the trend in the future may be moving toward more openness. As the first generation of children adopted from Korea is reaching adulthood, a voluntary adoption registry is being established in Korea to give adoptees a chance to be reunited with their birth families. As other countries become more familiar and educated concerning adoption and adopted children from these countries come of age, these countries too may implement increased openness in adoptions, giving adoptees a chance to search for their birth families.

Sometimes I am asked if I would ever like to trace my birth mother and meet her, and the answer is "No!" Oh, it's not that I do not ever think about her or have questions I might like answered. But I have lived with the reality of adoption every day of my life and am very comfortable talking about it. If I received a phone call or a knock on my door from my birth mother, it would not throw my world into a tailspin.

My entire family knows about my adoption and is very open about it. But that may not be the case with my birth family. When my birth mother placed me for adoption, she was assured of anonymity. I hope she finished college, married and had a family. I realize that it is entirely possible that she has never told her husband or children or those people close to her that she had a daughter when she was very young. If I were to contact her, it could be devastating for her. Given the chance that she still desires her anonymity, I will never try to enter her world. For a birth parent who desires anonymity, a closed adoption is an advantage.

For some people, the sealed records of a closed adoption are a source of safety. For others, they are a source of frustration. Before my dad passed away we had many conversations about my birth mother. In fact, one day he surprised me by questioning, "Honey, what would you want me to do if your birth mother came to our door?"

"Oh, Dad, you and Mom are my mom and dad. I'm not interested in looking her up," I said emphatically.

He persisted, "But wouldn't you want to meet her? If she came to us, you wouldn't be looking her up."

Wanting to please him, I finally said okay but asked why it seemed so important to him. "You've been wonderful," he said, "and I just want her to know how well you've turned out."

My dad never got the chance to meet my birth mother before he died, to express his gratitude for the joy we experienced as father and daughter. Many people are unable to share the words they long to share with the parents or children from whom they are separated because of closed records. For these, closed adoptions present a disadvantage in cutting off all interaction between birth families and adoptive families.

One day I was shopping at the mall with my tiny infant daughter peacefully asleep in her stroller. I stopped at least a half-dozen times as people "oo-ooed" and "ah-hhed" at her dark curls, blue eyes and long eyelashes. Overwhelmed with thankfulness to the mother of this beautiful baby girl, I spontaneously stopped and selected an engraved, heart-shaped, sterling silver locket for her. Later I chose a tiny picture of our darling daughter to glue inside. I wrapped it along with several other pictures I thought the mother might enjoy having. My unpremeditated act of gratitude for the daughter we share never reached my daughter's birth mother. I had no way of tracking her. But it has stayed on a shelf in my closet, a reminder of the bond I share with a woman I will most likely never know. Because information is closed, the locket will never serve its intended purpose.

Another adoptive mother recently sent us pictures and a letter for the birth mother of the twin sons she adopted internationally. In her letter she shared her own story of birthing twin boys who lived only a few hours. Then she told how, several years later, after much prayer for a baby boy, she and her husband were doubly surprised with the adoption of infant boy twins, birthed by this mother to whom she was writing. Mother-to-mother contact is so far unprecedented in the country where this adoption took place, but we will send her letter to the government officials and see whether they are willing to forward it to the birth mother. When closed records prevent the giving and receiving of gratitude between birth parents and adoptive families who might benefit from the contact, this secrecy can be a disadvantage.

Lack of medical records has in the past been another disadvantage in a closed adoption. I grew up without a scrap of medical history. I do not know if my family has any history of cancer, heart disease or mental illness. Every time I am seen as a new patient I simply have had to answer, "I don't know," when queried about my medical history. The lack of information has not been more than an annoyance because I have been healthy. But my lack of medical history will impact my biological children as well, for they only have history from their father's side of the family. For people with significant health problems, the sealed records of adoption can be life-threatening. Today medical history is given, whenever possible, even in a closed adoption.

Advantages and Disadvantages of Open and Semi-Open Adoption

Relatively few adoptions are totally open with both the complete disclosure of all identifying information and shared parenting of the child. It takes a unique and very mature relationship for shared adoptive/birth parenting to be successful. Some who have entered into a totally open adoption are advocates for its merits. For it to work, adoptive and birth families must have high self-esteem so that they are not at all threatened by each other. And the child must be able to handle two sets of parents. Families themselves must evaluate whether a totally open adoption is workable for them.

The great majority of adoptions are open in varying degrees according to the comfort level of the families. We received a call I will never forget from a pastor friend telling us he had a young woman in his office who was eight-and-a-half months pregnant. He went on to explain that she was the youngest in a family of five children. He had told her about our family, that we had four children. When she realized that if we adopted her baby that baby would be the youngest of five children, she said, "That's my family." I remember being thrilled with the news that we were probably going to have a new baby soon—and then feeling terrified at the request that we meet together with the birth parents and even some extended family.

I had lived with a closed adoption my whole life, and I

knew what to expect from it. But I did not know anything about an open adoption. I was not sure I wanted to. We did not immediately agree to the meeting. Rather, in the few days after the phone request we prayed for guidance and asked friends, including our attorney, for advice. No one encouraged us to meet together with the parents of our baby-to-be. Still, our pastor friend pressed, and finally, reluctantly, we agreed.

My lips were glued to my teeth with nervousness as we entered the meeting room. I willed my rigid body to relax as if it could respond on command, but I was terrified. I could neither make small talk nor smile. In contrast to my frightened state, I noticed my baby's birth mother sitting on a couch across the room, looking very pregnant, but relaxed and radiantly pretty, with shiny brown hair and an easy smile. She wore black maternity pants and blouse, and when she smiled, her cheeks revealed gorgeous dimples. She was so vivacious that she immediately set me at ease. I found myself riveted to her dancing eyes and animated personality. We also were given the delightful privilege to meet our baby's birth dad and maternal grandparents. With the pastor and staff mediating, we talked for over an hour about our backgrounds, about our shared hopes for this baby and even about my plans for decorating the nursery.

What special memories we store from that afternoon, which we can unwrap as needed when our little boy Mark asks about his background. Despite all of my apprehension, I will always look back on that meeting as one of the richest experiences of my life.

Before our meeting, I feared the unknown. I was worried that if I met my baby's birth parents they would want to interfere in our lives. In a sense, I looked at them as a hindrance to our baby, almost like extra weight to be cast off. I did not understand what a valuable gift my baby's family had offered to me by suggesting to share an afternoon together. I'm very thankful we did not refuse. We experienced firsthand the advantages of semi-open adoption, of sharing some contact with the birth parents of our baby.

Had I not had the privilege of meeting the parents of our baby, I would have harbored many unanswered questions in my heart, forever speculating about the truth. I know myself well enough to know that I would always have curiously wondered what Mark's birth parents looked like—silently picking strangers out of a crowd and pondering if they could be my little boy's parents.

I know this, because as a little girl my mother and I used to play a similar game. I remember riding up an escalator with my mother in a large downtown department store. As we rode, my mom and I noticed a unique birthmark on the calf of the woman who stood just ahead of us on the stairs. We noticed, because the colored pigmentation was almost a match to the birthmark I have on my own calf. My mom's eyes and mine locked, we started to giggle, and I whispered to her, "Maybe that's my birth mom!" We had many such instances as I was growing up, where some characteristic or expression in a total stranger would strike a familiar chord and my mind would fill with wonderment, speculating about whether I had really seen the woman who gave me birth.

Imagine the surprise I felt one evening when I attended an engagement party. The honored guest walked over to me and pointed to a woman across the living room, separated from me by perhaps seventy or eighty people, declaring, "Jorie, that woman over there looks like what I think you might look like in about twenty years. She looks like she's your mother!" I had no doubt as to whom he was referring. The resemblance was striking. "Maybe she is my mother," I answered truthfully. But I did not choose to speak to her. I don't think she was my birth mother, but I will never know.

The contacts Ron and I shared with Mark's birth family will keep us from such speculation, and to us they are a real advantage of semi-open adoption. We can tell Mark definite answers to many of his questions about his birth parents as he grows up. I can tell him where he gets his dancing eyes, engaging smile and vivaciousness, because in those areas he is a dead ringer for his birth mom.

We can also tell Mark with certainty where he got his crooked little finger. When he was born and we went to get our first glimpse of him in the hospital, we were met in the hallway by our baby's birth dad, a burly football player, who had just held his new little son for the first time. Filled with emotion which came from deep within him, tears freely flowing down his cheeks, this young birth father declared, "He has a crooked little finger, just like mine." And he held up his fingers to prove it. Not a day passes that I'm not reminded of Mark's birth dad when I see that unmistakably matching set of little fingers on our son. Instead of creating problems, the semi-openness we shared has been a rich legacy of information for our son.

Can a Child Be Taken Away?

Is a family's fear of a child being taken away by that child's birth parents a valid one? When an international adoption is completed overseas and the child is brought into the United States with a valid immigrant visa, there is virtually no chance that the child will be taken away. Impediments and complications can occur early in the process of an international adoption, but once a child is at home in the U.S. there is a high degree of security.

However, in domestic adoptions there are documented cases where birth parents have come back to reclaim their children with heartbreaking results for the adoptive parents. What can a family do to brace themselves for this reality? Becoming aware of adoption laws in the state in which you live and the state in which you are adopting is very important. In some states, the adoption laws are very "adoptive-parent friendly," and in others the laws are "birth-parent friendly." Some states protect both families' rights. If court cases in the state in which you live and or the state in which you adopt have overturned an adoption before, it is possible that it could happen again. A wise family will collect data so that they are informed.

In the state in which we are licensed, when a birth parent signs relinquishment statements and certificates of irrevocability, they are effective immediately. In other states, statutes may allow a birth parent six months, nine months or even longer in which to change their minds.

Relinquishment statements should always be signed by both of the birth parents. Without signed statements by both, the adoption is an at-risk adoption. The parent who did not sign could come back, object to the adoption and possibly overturn it. Families who want to protect themselves should choose professionals with whom to work who can make them aware of state statutes and regulations pertaining to adoption, who can help them understand birth-parent and adoptive-parent rights in their state, and who will seek relinquishment and consent papers signed by both birth parents before making a placement. While not a guarantee, these steps can dispel much of the fear a family might otherwise feel in pursuing a domestic adoption. This issue is addressed further in chapter ten.

Adoption Contract

A contract is a document most families draw up together outlining the degree of openness their adoption will have—how much contact there will be between birth parents and adoptive parents. Although the contract is usually mediated by a social worker or attorney, the birth mother is in the driver's seat in setting the parameters of the relationship. Adoptive families may feel this is an unfair advantage for the birth mother. The birth mother also possesses the authority to choose the family to whom she will entrust the privilege of parenting her child. If she does not like the relationship the adoptive family suggests, she will likely be allowed to choose another family.

The contract may spell out whether or not the adoptive family will share the birth experience in the hospital and how many times per year the birth mother may expect letters or pictures. She may specify whether she wants to give the baby some kind of keepsake from her or to have an "Entrustment Ceremony" to present the baby to the adoptive family. There may be a statement in the contract which specifies that if either of the parties wishes additional contact to that which has already been agreed upon, either party may contact a specified neutral party, and that by mutual consent they can add or change the agreement.

Presently only six states have laws allowing court enforcement of an openness agreement after the finalization of the adoption. Many birth mothers have been heartbroken because adoptive families cooperated in order to adopt the baby and then pulled away, realizing the agreement is not usually enforceable. I know of birth mothers who wait anxiously for the birthdays of their children and are depressed each day that passes if the promised pictures and letters are late or never arrive.

Court enforcement is no substitute for integrity. Families looking at an open adoption should not enter into one unless they are willing to honor the desires of the birth mother. The anniversaries and milestones are likely very important to her, and she deserves that respect for choosing to entrust her flesh and blood to an adoptive family.

Voluntary Adoption Registries

Voluntary search registries pertain to both open and closed adoptions. Adults who were adopted domestically can register in their state, verifying that they wish to be notified if a birth relative is searching for them. Birth parents can register as well, in case their children are trying to find them. Adoptive families are notified that this registry is available, as are birth parents when they relinquish their children. If both parties are seeking information about each other, a match is made. If only one party is seeking information, no information is made available to either. Search registries are a good solution, enabling contact between birth families and adoptive families regardless of whether an adoption was open or closed and despite promises made in an outdated contract. For some individuals a voluntary search registry is a lifeline to answers about their past. Search registries are currently available only in Korea and the U.S.

Building Trust

The biggest factor in open versus closed adoption seems to be trust between birth families and adoptive families. Families who want a closed adoption probably fear that birth parents will interfere with their parenting, and so they shrink from contact. Birth mothers who want the contact of an open or semi-open adoption fear that the family will not live up to the agreement and they will be cut off from their children. Adoptive parents have trouble trusting birth parents, and birth parents have trouble trusting adoptive parents. How can this trust be built so that the adoptive experience can be successful, whether it be open or closed?

One way to build trust is to share information, at least non-identifying information between birth families and adoptive families. Because we met our son's parents and realized we shared the same dreams and hopes for him, I have no worry that they will ever come and try to take him back. Once when he was a toddler doing something especially cute, one of our older sons exclaimed, "Mom, if his birth mom and dad saw how cute he was, they'd want him back." Although he was adorable, I knew that was not true. Marks birth parents had explained to us that they wanted to be very careful in choosing us so that they could delegate that task of parenting to us. Once they knew they could trust us, they explained that they didn't want to interfere. The birth mother told a mutual friend that she knows her son is where he is supposed to be. I have no fear because of the trust that was built between us as we got to know each other.

Praying for our own birth parents is another way of tearing down fears and building trust toward them. Although my own adoption was a closed one and I know little about my birth mother, I have prayed for her my whole life. My parents taught me that days that are very special milestones for me, like my birthday and Christmas, are milestones which may bring sadness to my birth mother. I pray especially for her on those days. Prayer is an effective way for us to show our concern, whether we participate in an open or closed adoption. I may not know where my children's birth parents are, but God does, and he can encourage them as I pray.

Finally, acknowledging that our adopted children have another set of parents, their biological parents, can help to build trust. Ignoring birth parents either mentally or physically does not erase them, like deleting them on a computer screen. All children who are adopted have birth parents, whether or not we want to acknowledge that fact. And we are bonded to those people in intangible ways for the rest of our lives because we share a common denominator, the child or children we love. The very least we can do is focus on the positive things about our children's birth parents: (1) They gave our children life, which in this day of easy abortion is a great gift. (2) They wanted better for that child than they themselves could provide. No decision to abandon a child or to place that child in an orphanage or adoptive home is an easy decision, no matter who the parents are. We can honestly say that that parent or those parents wanted better than he or she could provide. (3) They gave our children the legacy of characteristics we love about them—their enthusiasm, creativity, dimples or eyelashes.

We may not ever meet our children's birth parents face to face, but we know them, because we know their child. Let's focus on loving them because we love their child. My parents modeled a tremendous love and respect for my birth parents. I want to give my adopted children the same gift. Open versus closed adoption is of no consequence if I seek to promote understanding, love and trust toward the birth parents of my children.

6

GENETIC, MEDICAL AND EMOTIONAL FACTORS

When I am afraid, I will trust in you. In God,
whose word I praise, in God I trust;
I will not be afraid.
PSALM 56:3-4

W HEN ANDREA, OUR CURLY-HAIRED ANGEL AND FIRST
daughter, had been in our home for a few weeks, I listened to
a woman addressing families who, like ours, had adopted or
were contemplating adopting children living in orphanages
where medical care was minimal or nonexistent.

"Plan that your adopted child will have AIDS, and then if he
or she does not, you will be a very fortunate family," she
admonished.

Many families hearing those words that day did not go
through with adoption. The thought of bringing an undiag-
nosed or misdiagnosed and potentially life-threatening disease
home to an already established family was more risk than
many who heard those words were willing to take.

We already had taken the leap of faith and had adopted this
tiny dark-haired beauty, transporting her across an ocean into

our home for better or worse. Although we had discussed international medical risks including lack of records and accurate testing, unsanitary equipment and misdiagnosis, still this new warning alarmed me. We thought we had upturned every stone regarding medical issues and faced international adoption in a developing country with our eyes wide open. Once again the monster of fear strangled my heart.

I fixed lunch less than enthusiastically for my boys when I returned from the meeting. I felt burdened and overwhelmed by the weight of the risk to which Ron and I had perhaps unintentionally exposed our family. I decided to share some of the information I had heard with my children. I needed to talk and sincerely wanted to know what they thought.

"What would you want us to do if we discover that Andrea has AIDS?" I began. The boys loved it when I asked them serious questions; they felt a sense of importance when asked about adult topics. Their eyes widened momentarily as they pondered their responses. "Does she have it?" one asked. "Aren't we going to get to keep her?" probed another. My fifth- and second-graders were thinking. The conversation was too advanced for my four-year-old, but he listened with a worried look on his face. My twenty-one-month old was stuffing lunch into his mouth, oblivious to the seriousness of our conversation.

It was my serious, sensitive seventh-grader who spoke last. "Mom," he exhorted, "if Andrea has AIDS, that's all the more reason why we should have adopted her. No baby should have to die alone."

The depth of his maturity at that moment brought me back to reality. We had become educated regarding medical risks. We had done our best to provide the best available testing to determine her health. We had prayed for God to choose a child for us. And now we had to trust God, allowing Him to be God whatever the outcome.

I am not the only person who has worried about genetic and medical issues regarding adoption. Every family considering adoption must become familiar with the issues surrounding an adopted child's health. There are medical risks and medical unknowns for every child who is adopted.

Medical Unknowns and Risks

The medical histories that now accompany most domestically adopted children represent a huge advance in adoptive medicine. They will answer many questions and alleviate many risks. Most of the medical unknowns with which I have lived for my entire life are no longer mysteries for these families.

Advances in medical needs of internationally adopted children are progressing far more slowly. When a child is placed in an orphanage it is unlikely that a medical history will come along with him or her. It is impossible to obtain a medical history and family background on a child who is abandoned or deserted—or born to a single mother who enters a hospital under an assumed name and runs away after giving birth, leaving her child in the hospital.

Medical records on children housed permanently in orphanages are likely sporadic and sketchy. Hard-working orphanage staff have little time for record-keeping regarding childhood illnesses, immunizations, or even height and weight. Due to lack of information and records, most children adopted internationally will have many medical unknowns.

Children coming out of developing countries are often not tested for AIDS or Hepatitis B because of the difficulty of obtaining sanitary, sophisticated lab equipment. Conditions that we have come to expect as the norm regarding lab work and diagnoses may be impossible to reproduce in developing countries. If supplies like sterile needles, syringes, surgical tubing, collection vials, slides and refrigeration are not readily available to overseas medical personnel, they may not be trained to draw blood. If sterile supplies are not available and staff is not adequately trained to conduct testing, the test itself will be a greater risk to the children than not being tested at all.

In fact, conducting a lab test under inappropriate conditions can even expose the child to the very disease for which he or she is being tested. Since the risk of testing often puts children in jeopardy, extreme care must be taken when making the decision whether or not to do tests at all. Often it is simply not worth the risk. Yet lack of testing will create more medical unknowns for children adopted internationally.

A wise alternative might seem to be to send supplies and physicians acquainted with lab procedures to draw blood and conduct the necessary testing. We know of families who have requested this alternative to obtain the results they were seeking. This procedure is possible. But since lab equipment is large and not portable, once the blood is drawn it would need to be refrigerated and flown to another country, to a large city with a full-service lab, in order for the tests to be completed. In some areas of the world costs to do such testing would add dramatically to already expensive adoption costs.

In addition, health screening is a very sensitive issue in any country where adoption agencies and adoptive families are present as guests of the government. Sending in physicians from home is not often a feasible solution.

Sometimes health practices in a developing country put a child at risk. The widespread belief that intramuscular transfusions of blood would improve the health of children caused whole orphanages in one country to be inoculated with blood. Since the same needle was often used over and over and the blood used was unknowingly infected with the HIV virus, whole orphanages of children were unwittingly infected with AIDS.

Some areas of the world have higher instances of certain illnesses than others, and adoptive families need to be aware of these statistics when selecting a country from which to adopt. Some countries or whole sections of countries have no documented instances of AIDS. The chances of adopting a child infected with the HIV virus from these countries is not very high even if the child has not been tested. Still, there are no guarantees. In parts of the world where drug use and prostitution are common or where there are many documented cases of the disease in the general public, the risk of AIDS should be carefully evaluated.

In Asia hepatitis B is more prevalent than in the West. Some infectious disease experts estimate that the instance of hepatitis B is as high as 10 percent. Families adopting in this part of the world need to be aware that their adoptive child could be infected. In the west, Fetal Alcohol Syndrome is of more concern due to high alcohol consumption. Education regarding abstinence from alcohol during pregnancy is slow to penetrate long-standing social patterning. Young babies with Fetal Alcohol Syndrome are hard to diagnose; families adopting from countries with this problem need to be willing to take the risk that their child could be affected.

A change in U.S. immigration law, effective July 1, 1997, requires all immigrants to have up-to-date immunizations before entering the U.S.A. This legislation was not meant to affect orphan children, but according to the law as written, all orphans entering the U.S. are required to have current immunizations for mumps, measles, rubella, polio, tetanus and diphtheria toxoids, pertussis, influenza type b (Hib), hepatitis B, varicella, pneumococcal and influenza.

The ramifications of this law pose a risk to some adoptable

children. For many in fragile health, the act of immunization may give them the very disease they are being immunized against. These children would benefit from waiting until they are in their new homes and their pediatricians feel they are in good enough health to withstand the immunizations without risk. Others may be immunized with serum, needles or syringes of questionable cleanliness or quality because of lack of availability. Since in many areas of the world immunization of children is not a widespread practice, vaccines, syringes and needles are sometimes difficult to obtain. It is uncertain what effect this law will have on children adopted internationally.

Medical Inaccuracies

Another medical issue is that sometimes medical information given on adoptive children is inaccurate. We know of children who were tested for AIDS and hepatitis B whose results were invalid. Sometimes lack of proper nutrition or the incubation period of the disease can cause a false negative or false positive test reading, gravely misleading those who are basing their decision for adoption on test results. Human error is also a common problem in lab work. How sad that a child might lose his or her chances for adoption because someone inadvertently made a mistake on a lab test. And it is equally unfortunate when a lab report fails to catch the disease it was intended to screen.

In many parts of the world, the general public will more readily approve of the international adoption of children with medical problems. Because of this sentiment, medical reports may exaggerate a condition or even declare a condition which the child does not have, in order to give that child a chance to be adopted internationally.

The medical report of one of the first children we placed for

adoption from a certain country stated that she had a hole in
her heart. Her parents were willing to take her, medical condition and all. They took her to several specialists after her
adoption. None could find anything wrong with her heart.
Several years later she is a happy, strong, active child.

Another child's medical report indicated that he had a type
of muscular dystrophy. His parents took a huge risk in adopting him. Yet when the family arrived home and their pediatrician examined him and conducted appropriate tests, nothing
showed up. This child is a healthy, normal boy.

As the world grows in understanding of the merits of adoption, perhaps this practice of exaggerated medical reports will
diminish. Adoptive parents need to be aware that inaccurate
medical reports sometimes occur, recognizing that a medical
report is but one piece of information on an adoptive child.
The report may or may not be valid and should be neither
overvalued or underestimated.

Sometimes a government will expedite the quick adoption
of a particular child, living in one of their orphanages, who
has a medical condition they are unable to treat in their country. In one such case a child had a congenital orthopedic problem that required several surgeries which were impossible in
her own country. Authorities were very cooperative so that the
child could receive treatment. The family was informed of the
condition and had made application for treatment in a children's hospital before she came home to the United States.

The authorities in the country allowing this adoption have
followed the case with much interest for several years. They
have documented the child's progress with stories and pictures
in the local newspaper. Even the most adamant objectors to
intercountry adoption seem to support an adoption where the
child receives treatment for an otherwise untreatable condition.

Once several of our staff were on a train overseas, escorting international children who were to be adopted in the United States. Tensions began to rise in the train car in which we were riding when the local people noticed we were caring for their national children. However, when our overseas staff explained that the children were going to the United States to new families to receive treatment, everyone relaxed and the tension went away.

Genetic Issues in Adoption

Some families considering adoption worry about a child's genetic background, wondering how much influence it will have over what the child will become. Will it be a child's *background* or *parenting* that determines who he or she becomes? The answer will probably be some of both.

Every child we parent, whether biological or adopted, comes as a gift to us. As I understand my role in parenting, I see my role as twofold. First, it is my job to open that gift and enjoy the package that was entrusted to me. Each child is unique, with different talents and personalities. That is my child's genetic make-up—that delightful package of surprises that I will keep on opening and enjoying for the rest of my life. Each of my seven children has a special genetic make-up different from his or her siblings. Each will blossom with talents that are his or hers alone—including ones which could not possibly have been inherited from my husband or me! We have been thrilled, for example, with our adopted son's perfect pitch—both musically and in baseball.

The atmosphere that I create in my home for my children is their environment. I can use my unique parenting skills to help each of those children become all that they were created to be. That tempering and encouraging will take every ounce of strength and creativity that I can put forth as a mother. That is my second role in parenting.

Will my adopted children have any negative genetic traits? Bad genes? They may, but so may my birth children. One privilege we as parents have is that we can help our children focus on developing their most positive qualities, to bring out the best in them.

A study completed on adopted children by the Search Institute in Minneapolis, Minnesota, in 1994 should be encouraging to any family considering adoption, giving strong indication that a child's environment and parenting are very strong influences on them. This study, the largest ever completed on adopted children in the United States, investigated adolescents who had been adopted as infants. (Children adopted when they are older would not be expected to test with exactly the same results. Although children who are adopted when they are older can adjust beautifully, still, the younger the child is when he or she is adopted, the greater the chance for success.)

Citing just one aspect of the study, the adopted youths were compared to non-adopted youths regarding general indicators of well-being. In school, 62 percent of the adopted youth had a B average or better compared to 53 percent of nonadopted youth. In the area of connectedness, 83 percent of the adopted youth had three or more friends compared to 78 percent of nonadopted youth. In the dimension of caring, 71 percent of the adopted youth placed high personal value on helping other people compared to 48 percent of the nonadopted youth. Comparing optimism, 74 percent of adopted youth expected to be happy ten years from now versus 68 percent of nonadopted youth. Studying self-concept, 55 percent of the adopted youth expressed high self-esteem compared to 45 percent of nonadopted youth. And evaluating support, 83 percent of adopted youth experienced a high level of parental support versus 68 percent of nonadopted youth.[1]

Adopted children have shown that they can achieve as significantly as those who are not. As a matter of fact, adopted children have become presidents of the United States, Olympic gold medalists and founders of multimillion-dollar corporations. Gerald Ford, ice skater Scott Hamilton and Wendy's fast-food-chain president Dave Thomas were all adopted children.

Lack of Emotional Development

Sometimes children who have been living in orphanages are slow in their emotional development. I will never forget the strange lack of noise in some of the orphanages we visited overseas. The silence was foreboding.

For a month after we brought Andrea home, she never cried. "A perfect baby!" you might exclaim. And she was a delight. The first night we had her in our home, after all the excitement at the airport, I was not looking forward to getting up at night again with a new baby. Because she was not quite four months old, I expected to get up several times to feed her—surely she wouldn't yet sleep through the night.

I woke up to total silence at three a.m. Bolting out of bed, I wondered if I could possibly have slept through her cries. Worse, I shuddered involuntarily: *I hope nothing serious has happened to her!* When I entered the nursery I could see by the dim glow of the night light that she was awake. Her large eyes seemed even larger in the half-light. But even in a strange room, with strange smells and strange sights, she didn't cry. She did not cry when she was wet, tired or hungry. She simply did not cry. Somehow, in her young life, she had learned that no one had time to come to her when she cried, and so she learned not to. It was a moment of celebration for our family when Andrea finally learned to cry.

Some children are confined to an institution as their universe, a room or crib as their world. Children without much stimulation or human contact may have emotional or developmental delays. Crying is a normal human response, but if caregivers are so stressed from overwork that they are unable to respond to a child's cries, the child will stop crying.

In some countries, economic conditions are so poor that staff is paid to work only during the day. If at 6:00 in the evening the orphanage doors are locked and all the workers go home except for the night watchman, the children will learn it is useless to cry at night.

Walking up and down the rows of children in several orphanages able to provide only minimal care, I noticed that children had a variety of responses to me. Some reached up to me with both arms outstretched, hoping I would pick them up. Others ignored me, silently rocking back and forth in their cribs, mimicking the motion of being cradled in a rocking chair, but oblivious to me. Still others, when I approached their cribs, recoiled from my touch shielding their faces with a hand and forearm, in that position which has come to be known as the orphan salute.

Many of these developmentally deprived children, when given love and appropriate emotional and physical stimulation, will catch up, while others have given up and shrink back permanently from a world that has failed to give them the support they need to thrive. An adopted child who has been living in an institutional environment, regardless of the conditions, should be given time to bond, to adjust, to make up for all the developmental stimulation that he or she may have missed.

One articulate seven-year-old girl was adopted internationally after living her entire life in orphanages. She shocked her mother one day by asking to buy a baby bottle when they were shopping. Unashamedly she told her mother she needed to drink from it because she couldn't remember having one. For several days this wise mother cuddled her daughter as she drank from a bottle, making up for lost time.

Not all children will be so in touch with their needs. But a wise parent will patiently give adopted children opportunities to make up for losses in their lives. Children are sometimes developmentally delayed several years or even permanently from institutionalization.

Attachment Disorder

Often families contemplating adoption have heard the term "attachment disorder," and it frightens them very much. In this condition, over which there is much professional disagreement, children are described as having trouble forming loving, intimate relationships. At its worst, a child with this disorder appears to have almost no ability to be affectionate. He or she may also have little conscience and may not be able to trust others. Although this condition is not exclusively related to adopted children, adopted children sometimes appear to have the disorder.[2] While the theory may be somewhat controversial, the truth is that when children have been deprived of love and or physical necessities, some of them will withdraw and become unable to learn to give and receive love and to trust others, even when a loving, stable environment is provided for them.

Although the problem of attachment disorder will potentially be more prevalent with children adopted when they are older, still it can occur with children adopted as infants. One mother was at her wit's end with a son she adopted domestically as an infant. He had most recently stolen a whole case of breath mints—which, was in itself frustrating to his mother. Then he had pulverized package after package of these breath mints in his mother's food processor until they were the con-

sistency of fine powder. He was discovered peddling packages of this fine white powder at his grade school, passing it
off as cocaine. When confronted about this or any other incidence in his life, he was not repentant or remorseful. He simply did not seem to have a conscience. He was diagnosed
with attachment disorder.

Another family adopted a darling daughter internationally.
This little girl constantly acted as though she feared that there
would not be enough food for her to eat, stealing whatever
she was able to find in the kitchen. Her family began uncov-
ering stashes of food hidden in unusual places around the
house. One day her mother discovered a five-pound bag of
flour underneath a chair in the living room. Another day this
mother spied three empty granola bar packages and over
twenty crumpled candy wrappers peeking out from beneath
the couch.

As time went on it was not unusual for the parents to find
dozens of apple cores hidden in drawers, sticky remains of
entire jars of jam removed from the pantry and cast aside
empty behind family room draperies, or plastic packaging
from devoured cheese or lunch meat camouflaged among
packages of plastic sandwich bags and brown paper sacks in
the kitchen drawer.

And this little girl's hoarding was not limited to food items. On
her foraging escapades she would scour every room of the
house for useful trinkets and store them in her room. Although
nothing she took was valuable, nothing in the home was safe.
This child excavated items deliberately hidden in bottoms of
closets and on out-of-reach shelves. When confronted about her
stealing, the child consistently lied, instead of confessing the
truth. Sometimes children who have experienced early depriva-
tion have a hard time learning to trust anyone but themselves.

Other children who have had minimal love and attention

have a difficult time learning to give and receive love. I have seen babies arch their backs, almost lunging out of the arms of people wanting to cuddle them, because they have not been used to close physical contact. Others try to physically or emotionally hurt themselves or the very people who have chosen to love them.

Some children need a lifetime of consistent love, patience and discipline to give them a chance to learn to build trusting relationships. Some of these children will make more progress than others. Families whose children struggle with attachment and bonding may benefit from an outside system of understanding friends and professionals who can encourage and support them, so that they will not feel personally responsible for their child's unmet needs.

One mother who has lived with the reality of attachment disorder for nineteen years, having adopted a child who lived in an orphanage for six months with severe neglect before she was adopted, shared with me the following insight gleaned from her years of experience:

Adopting a child (baby or older) who has suffered abuse or neglect takes stouthearted parents. We need to be clear that we can't depend on this child to meet our love needs. We need to stay detached enough to know that if the child rages, the rage may be directed at us but it's not really about us—it's about that early unresolved pain. The love we give, by itself, will never be enough to heal the child. It's as if her (or his) heart has a hole in it, so the love we pour in drains right out. It helps to remember that this is God's child more than ours, and God is a healer. He is the one who can plug up that hole and make the child capable of being nourished by our love and his.

But for every child who exhibits behavior showing that he or she has been wounded emotionally, affecting his or her ability to form loving and trusting relationships, a far greater number of children are resilient, flexible and able to bond strongly with their new families. Story after story of happy adoptive families will overwhelmingly attest to this fact. Still, it is wise for families contemplating adoption of children who have been abused or neglected to be aware of potential problem areas. And it is important to pray specifically for the child's emotional well-being, healing for damage that may have already occurred, blessing on that child, and God's special insight for you as parents to know how best to help this child become all that God intended for him or her to be.

The Issue of Grief in Adoption

Many children feel a sense of loss as they are uprooted from the only surroundings they know and are brought to a new home. It may be hard for some families to understand this feeling when they know that they are providing a life of wonderful opportunity and privilege compared to that which the child left behind. But children will not have the sophistication or perspective to see the long-term benefits of our love. They will only know the reality of being uprooted from everything that is familiar to them, and they will feel that loss. They may miss a favorite caregiver or friend in the orphanage. They may miss the repetition of a routine that gave them a sense of stability day after day. They may miss familiar sounds, smells and tastes that were part of their world. And taken from that world, they may grieve. I have come to realize that children of all ages can grieve.

The best Christmas gift I have ever received was the birth of our second daughter, Cam, on Christmas day 1995. She was born halfway around the world across an ocean in Asia, and I was able to pick her up when she was four weeks old. Sometimes people comment that a Christmas birthday will be overlooked, but I was thrilled. Besides sharing her birthday with the celebration of Jesus' birth, as the youngest of seven children in our family she has the best chance of having most of her siblings home to celebrate her birthday on Christmas.

The arrivals of each of my children have been the highlights of my life next to my wedding day. Whether in the delivery room, hospital or airport or on foreign soil, each has been a thrilling experience. Cam's "Handing Over" ceremony was no exception. I felt she was my very first baby all over again. She was passed around and kissed by caregivers and nurses in the maternity hospital where she was born. She was held by government officials as we signed the adoption papers, and we captured it all on camera in dozens of "Kodak moments."

But when night fell and the day's festivities ended, Cam was a different baby. Amber, a friend and fellow social worker, had accompanied me on the trip. Amber and I tried to settle her down for bed, Cam began to scream. And she did not stop screaming. In fact, she screamed inconsolably all night long. It wasn't just a cry. As a mother of seven I wouldn't have been concerned about a cry. But Cam screamed the way my other babies have screamed only when they were in the doctor's office and have received their immunizations. I began to wonder if I had made a mistake adopting this baby.

Amber and I tried everything two experienced mothers could think of, which included secrets from a raising a combined total of nine children and more than twenty-five years of parenting between us. We had an additional advantage in that we are both relaxed with babies. But nothing worked.

We finally came to the conclusion that Cam was angry. We did not look like anything she had ever seen in her life. (We are both blond.) We did not smell like anything she had ever smelled in her life. Our fragrances from soaps and shampoo gave our clothes, skin and hair far different scents than those to which she was accustomed. We did not sound like anything she had ever heard before. All our words of comfort in English must have sounded strange to her. At four weeks of age, Cam had had her whole world suddenly turned upside down, and we believe she sensed the difference and felt a loss.

During those first days she had many episodes of screaming inconsolably. Sometimes she would scream until her voice became hoarse.

Shortly after we got home the crying episodes subsided and she began to bond with us, her new family. In fact, once that bonding started Cam didn't want to be out of my sight, night or day. Therefore, until she was nearly six months old I nearly always wore her in a baby front pack. It was as though she was saying, "I lost my mother once. I don't want to lose another one!"

A feeling of loss can be experienced by a child at any age. Sometimes children will not grieve until they are adolescents; then they daydream about who they would have been if things had worked out differently and they had grown up with their birth parents. This introspection may evoke feelings of sadness for the parents they were not able to know.

Other children demonstrate their grief over "losing the life that could have been" or losing everything familiar to them through anger. One of the worst tantrums I have ever witnessed occurred in an international airport while I was escorting a child home to her new adoptive parents. In a sudden burst of outrage she threw herself on the floor, in the middle of a room packed with people, kicking and screaming out obscenities in her native language. I suppose I should be thankful that I did not speak her language so I didn't know exactly what she said, but I was told she had a lot to say—both to and about everyone! Several years later this young girl runs to give me a hug whenever I have the pleasure of seeing her, and she is a joy to her family, but her adoptive parents had several very challenging months of adjustment.

Leaving all familiarity behind and facing a life full of unknowns can be a terrifying. Some children are able to make peace with this loss much more easily than others. Putting ourselves in their shoes becomes an important exercise for those who are enduring the adjustment period with them, trying to understand and help.

How do we reconcile medical, emotional and genetic unknowns in adoptive parenting? Are there simply too many risks to embark on such an adventure? Each family must, of course, make their own decision regarding adoption. Even though you become aware of the issues involved, even though you choose professionals who are doing their best to address medical issues, even though you are praying for God to lead you to a child who will fit into your home, still there are no guarantees. But no birth child is delivered with a guarantee tied to his or her leg either!

Remember that God cares about your family, that he cares about the child who is placed in your home, and that he will give you insight into how to best parent that child. God is our only security and our best guarantee.

7

CROSSRACIAL ISSUES IN ADOPTION

There is neither Jew nor Greek, slave nor free,
male nor female, for you are all one in Christ Jesus.
GALATIANS 3:28

THE LAST VISIT I HAD WITH MY FATHER BEFORE HE DIED IS ONE which holds bittersweet memories for me. Since my husband and I and our children live on the West Coast and my parents live in the Midwest, we do not get to see each other as often as we wish we could. The yearly visits at Christmas and in summer which had been our pattern for many years suddenly ceased when my father took several falls and was no longer able to travel to our home or to our favorite spot on Lake Michigan. Knowing his health was failing, I longed to see him. I also longed to introduce him to his youngest granddaughter, our seven-month-old Asian baby girl, Cam. I decided to travel to see my mom and dad, taking our thirteen-year-old son, Luke, and the baby. Our few days together were meaningful to us all.

After visiting my dad one evening, my mother, Luke, Cam

and I met one of the other patients, a man with severe memory loss, sitting in his wheel chair in the hallway outside of my dad's room. We greeted him and noticed that he seemed especially interested in the baby. After gazing intently at my obviously Asian baby for many seconds, he announced, "She looks *so* Norwegian!" We are not sure what thoughts were occurring in this elderly Scandinavian man's mind as he spoke, but we were both flattered and amused. Wouldn't it be nice if the whole world was so oblivious to racial differences? What issues are of special concern to us as we consider the adoption of a child of a race different from our own?

Preparing People Around Us

One of my children does not respond well to surprises or sudden changes in plans, whether good or bad. I seriously doubt that we will ever mastermind a surprise birthday party for this son because by the time he got used to the idea, the party would be over! He needs time to ponder. He needs time to prepare. He is a thinker and enjoys lead time. He's definitely not someone on whom you want to try out a new "whoopie cushion." Someday I will entrust these facts with my future daughter-in-law.

This son has many kindred spirits in this world, those others who respond better to forewarning than to shock! Discussing adoption plans with family and friends and neighbors is a wise investment in our adopted child's future, especially when the child we plan to adopt is of a different racial heritage than ours. Out of respect and love for extended family and friends it is wise to take the extra time necessary to discuss with them your desire to adopt a child who will look significantly different than you. Explaining how you reached your decision will help them to feel more comfortable with your choice.

The generation before ours is often not as comfortable with racial differences as are many of us. Generations of societal patterning change slowly. Many of our parents and grandparents have never personally known anyone of a different race. For them it is a big step to think of having a grandchild or great-grandchild from such a different background. They will appreciate time to get used to the idea.

I had such a conversation with my father when Ron and I were intending to adopt an Asian baby. I always seek my parents' blessings on our plans. Although I could not have predicted his repines, he did not disappoint me. He expressed fatherly concern over whether another child would be too much work for me. But he ended our conversation by affirming, "I've learned not to worry about you any more. You always make good decisions." We received the blessing we sought.

What should a family do if their extended family, friends or neighbors object to their plans to adopt a crossracial child? Should they forsake their plans? This kind of decision is a very personal matter for each family to resolve.

Many years ago now our family received a phone call on a Friday afternoon from an attorney friend asking us if we would like to adopt a newborn biracial baby girl. What a tizzy that phone call started! Since she was already born we had only hours in which to make our decision. Ron and I wanted to adopt this baby. We wanted both boys and girls in our home, and we saw this as a wonderful opportunity to parent a precious little girl. But after much prayer during the weekend we decided to say, no.

Until the phone call we had never thought about the possibility of adopting a biracial baby. Consequently we had never spoken to our families, close friends or neighbors regarding this issue either. We felt that out of respect for our closest relationships we needed more time than we had to adequately prepare them.

Does that mean that families need permission from friends, neighbors and family before adopting a biracial or crossracial child? No. We know of an extended family who was 100 percent opposed to their children's adoption plans. Their first reply when the young couple expressed their longing to adopt was, "You're not planning to bring home that trash, are you?" The couple was shattered because they wanted the support of their extended family.

After much prayer and reflection the couple went ahead with the adoption even without the affirmation they desired from their extended family. They determined they could bring honor to God by loving a little child who needed parents and wholeheartedly wanted to do so. They did not agree with their parents' appraisal.

Initially they had rough sledding. The first time the parents met the young couple for dinner with their newly adopted son, they did not even acknowledge that their daughter had a baby in her arms. They ignored the baby, acting as if he was invisible. Instead of confronting their parents' lack of love, the younger couple decided to bathe the situation in prayer, realizing they were completely powerless to change their parents' attitudes. Gradually these grandparents softened their attitude toward their adopted grandson and this little boy began to grow in their hearts. Now, many years later, they love him as they love their flesh and blood. Our world changes slowly, one person at a time.

Keeping Cultural Heritage Alive

A special privilege and responsibility of adopting a crossracial, crosscultural child is to help that child keep his or her cultural and racial heritage alive. Authorities who grant permission to crossracial or crosscultural adoptions want to know that the children will grow up knowing who they are. Countries releasing their needy children for adoption want them to have a sense of identity rooted in their racial and cultural backgrounds.

How can families seek to give their children roots in a cultural and racial background different than their own? For parents who adopt their children as infants, all responsibility for teaching them about their country of origin falls on their shoulders. The way that children feel about their cultural and racial background will depend largely on how the parents feel about their children's background themselves.

The morning after Ron brought Andrea home to the United States from Eastern Europe, I brought her to church for the very first time. She was welcomed in every sort of way by kind greetings and words of thankfulness to God for answering our prayers for a safe trip across the ocean. Many people had a part in her life because our whole congregation prayed for her. I thanked them all for their faithfulness in supporting us in prayer. One woman said without thinking, "When she starts to speak, will she speak her native language?"

To which I replied, "Not unless we teach it to her!"

Just as our children will speak the language we model to them, they will view their country, culture, and race of origin the way we view them. They will take their cues from us.

If we are uncomfortable parenting a child of a different race, our child will be uncomfortable with his or her racial background. If we have negative feelings toward a country because of a political persuasion or because of the side they were on in a war, our child will grow up with negative feelings toward his or her country. These negative feelings will cause conflict in our child's life. A parent looking at crossracial or crosscultural adoption must look carefully at his or her own feelings on the subject before proceeding.

A family who takes time to study the country of origin of their adopted child is giving that child a gift. All countries have a rich and colorful culture which takes on new meaning when we realize we are learning about our child's relatives. A parent who builds appreciation for the child's background will help instill in that child a feeling of self-respect.

I have saved newspaper clippings about the countries from which our daughters came. Some day when they are older, as they show interest, I have all kinds of information for them which I store in containers we call Treasure Boxes. Some families have read books, studied the holidays, and learned about the customs and food of their children's countries.

Other families enjoy celebrating national holidays of their child's country of origin along with the holidays in the U.S.. We know parents who have spent much time studying the language spoken in their child's native land. Another set of parents employs a tutor to keep their two adopted daughters, who were adopted as grade schoolers, fluent in their native tongue.

Still others enjoy learning to prepare special foods and serving them on festive occasions. Children may enjoy trips to the library to check out children's stories written about children growing up in their country of origin as well as reading folk tales from their culture. Often families will buy mementos for their child when they travel to the country to pick them up. These objects can be hands-on tools to build cultural heritage when our children are young as well as keepsakes to treasure when our children are older.

One mother who enjoys sewing bought the fabric for her baby's christening gown from the country where her baby was born. This will some day be a cherished reminder of this child's country of origin.

I am often asked by prospective parents if they should keep the name given to their child before coming to the United States. Personal preference should be the deciding factor. In both of our international adoptions we chose to keep at least a portion of the name our girls were given. Our older girl's birth mother chose her name, and, since so many changes were going on in our daughter's life, we decided her name was one thing we could keep. However, our decision was made primarily because we liked her name, Andrea. If we had not liked her name, or if her name could have been a source of ridicule to her because it sounded so different from most American names, we would have changed it. We kept a portion of our younger daughter Cam's name, though it was not given by her mother. Some families do not choose to keep any portion of their child's name, but they still will have reminders of it in their child's passport or adoption papers. Other families use their child's name as a middle name. Names can be a positive link to our children's cultural heritage.

Some special-interest groups and adoption agencies provide picnics, Christmas parties or play groups as reunions for families who have adopted children from a certain country. These get-togethers can be a sharing of information between families who share a common bond. Many families enjoy sharing adoption stories with others who can identify and understand. Orphans Overseas has organized such events for families whom we have helped adopt.

A trip to our children's countries of origin can be a valuable link to their identity at a time when they are old enough to appreciate it. Until then, pictures or videos taken at the time our child was picked up can be used as a part of his or her history. One mother recounted to me that she took her daughter to South America to visit her country of birth the summer her daughter was sixteen. Although the daughter expressed ambivalence when they snapped pictures in front of the hospital where she was born and at the orphanage where she had lived, when they returned home the adoptive mother catalogued the pictures into an album for her daughter—and that album has become a valued reminder of a place the daughter now declares she loves. She has added national flags and keepsakes to her room, all part of her expression of her identity.

All the activities I have mentioned are tools which we can use to help keep our children's cultural and racial heritages alive. But in doing this, it is important as parents to always ask ourselves the question, "Whose interest am I serving?" Our goal is to help our children feel positive about themselves, to give them a positive identity even when that identity is different from our own.

Some families will implement all of the ideas to help keep their child's cultural and racial heritage alive. Others will pick and choose. Some activities will work at one point in a child's life, and others will need to be on hold. If your child likes exploring stories about his or her country, then the activity is a wise choice. If eating ethnic food is something the whole family enjoys, it should be continued.

If an activity is serving my needs as a parent more than the needs of my child, perhaps I need to stop the activity for a time, resuming it when I know my child is ready. When our older daughter was a baby, I organized several picnics and Christmas parties for families who had adopted children from the same country. Sharing common stories and seeing the children together was enjoyable for us all.

But as a parent who has multiple children by birth and adoption I soon recognized that at this time in our family's life it is more important for my children to blend as a family than to be focusing on their differences. Right now these children all need to be Kincaids. At some time I may resume these reunions. But when I do, I will once again ask myself the question, "Whose best interest am I serving by doing this?" All adoptive families need to ask themselves the same question and make choices based on those things which would most benefit their child.

Facing the World with Grace

Every time I leave the privacy of our home with my Asian daughter, it is as though we are wearing an announcement that we are an adoptive family. Since I have lived with the reality of adoption every day of my life, I am very comfortable sharing my experience and I don't mind when people ask me questions. But not everyone who adopts feels that comfortable. For an adoptive family relationship in a crossracial adoption to be successful, the family participating must feel very comfortable with adoption, since there is no way to hide the truth.

I can remember meeting new people, as I was growing up, and being pleasantly surprised when they unwittingly told me that I resembled my mom. She and I would go home and giggle together over the concealed truth of my adoption. After all, I do share many of my mom's mannerisms after living with her for so many years.

Ron and I are amazed at the unusual likeness between our four birth sons and our one adopted son. I used to comment that I have never seen another baby that looked more like our biological children than our fifth son. This similarity has been a source of joy to our family. And our older daughter, with her dark hair and blue eyes, looks like her daddy, a fact which enraptures them both.

In contrast, although our entire family is smitten with love for our Asian daughter, we will probably never find a physical likeness which will delude people on the street into thinking she is our biological child. Do we care? No! We cherish her and treasure the privilege of having an Asian daughter. But families adopting crossracially have to be ready to respond to the reality that everyone, including family, friends and total strangers, will know that the child you love is not your biological child.

In preparation for a crossracial adoption, it is wise to anticipate situations you may encounter with your child and plan what you will say. Some of us think on our feet better than others, and advance preparation can help us handle potentially awkward situations gracefully. A helpful rule that I try to always keep in mind is, No matter what people ask or say, *never be sarcastic!*

Sometimes you may feel people are rude. People may ask questions you feel are intrusive. Sometimes you will be tired and will not want anyone to ask you anything. But if you do not remember anything else, remember that our children are watching us and listening to us when we respond to questions and comments about them.

If we are sarcastic, our children will hear that tone of voice and feel the attitude behind it. If we are angry or defensive in our responses, our children will feel that angry and defensive spirit. If we are embarrassed, looking at adoption as second-best, our child will feel that attitude straight down to his or her toes. Even if that sarcasm, anger, defensiveness or embarrassment is not directed at our children, they will be taking their cues about how to feel about themselves and their adoption from you and how you talk about it with strangers.

They will model our attitudes. If we want our children to feel positive about their racial and cultural backgrounds, we as parents need to model grace and forgiveness to those who are insensitive and who lack understanding in their comments and questions.

I have made a personal commitment that no matter what people ask me about our adoptions, I will always tell the truth. But while I always seek to be truthful, I do not feel it is always necessary to tell every person I meet every intimate detail of our family's private life or every detail of my children's adoption stories. I have the privilege of discerning how much I will reveal and what I will choose to keep private.

I will certainly be more open with a close friend than I will with a clerk in the grocery store. If I am tired after a long day of writing home studies, watching swimming and gymnastics lessons and chauffeuring kids, and I quickly duck into the grocery for milk just moments before my hungry husband and older sons return for dinner, I will not recount as many of my feelings on adopting crossracially as when I am relaxed and not time-pressured.

I always want to be polite. I always seek to be positive. I always want people to go away feeling like adoption is wonderful. But I have the privilege and responsibility to decide what I will tell.

Sometimes I choose to simply say, "She's adopted," without offering further explanation. But I also clearly remember the sheer delight I felt as a child when my mother would occasionally ignore mentioning that I was adopted and people would assume I was her biological child. Although I am not at all embarrassed to be an adoptive mother, still I, too, have enjoyed the times when it has been assumed that my adopted children are biological. I am particularly tickled when this happens with my Asian child, who bears no physical resemblance to me, her mom!

As a minority person in several cities I visited on the way home with our new Asian daughter, I got many curious stares and questions about how it came to be that I, a Caucasian, was carrying a newborn Asian baby. Committed to my principle of telling the truth, I wanted to answer their questions but I did not always want to go into detail with every person I met. I began to discern a pattern to their questions. Usually the first question after they made eye contact was, "Is that your baby?"

"Yes," I always answered truthfully. Then their eyes would open wider, usually regarding me with a quizzical look, both probing for more information and hungry for the story. Sometimes I took the time to describe for them my joy and privilege in adopting this tiny dark-haired beauty. Other times, I would confirm just as truthfully, "Her father is Asian," and they would nod their heads knowingly, presumably thinking I was married to an Asian man. After all, our daughter's father *is* Asian. What I did not always disclose to total strangers was the reality that her *mother* is Asian too. Honesty, sometimes sprinkled with a sense of humor, can go a long way in showing grace to a world that is perhaps not as comfortable with crossracial adoption as are we.

Connecting to Our Crossracial Child

Realizing that we look very different physically from our child of a different race, what is the glue that will bind us together as parent and child? That question seems relevant only at the beginning investigation of crossracial adoption. Our Asian daughter does not carry a physical family resemblance to our Scandinavian-Scottish-Irish blend, with her silky, straight black hair and gorgeous almond eyes. But during her young life we have connected with her in countless ways that are far more important than looks alone. She is clearly left-handed, a fact that gives her left-handed eldest brother pleasure. Unlike all our other babies, whose first word was "Dada," Cam said, "Momma!"—electrifying me, her mother. She exhibits such a strong preference to all eight of us in our family that she has nearly defined the meaning of bonding. She pats us on the back and lays her head on our shoulders, and we know we are a family. I have teasingly said that she thinks she is blond!

We entered into a crossracial adoption with our eyes wide open. We admit that by adopting our Asian daughter we have altered the course of our family forever. We are now a multi-ethnic, multiracial family, and we have no question that by becoming such we have a chance to bring honor to God in a way we might never otherwise have experienced. We did not adopt our daughter to make a statement to the world. We adopted her because we knew we had enough love in our hearts and we wanted to share that love with another child.

Just weeks after our daughter arrived home, she became very seriously ill with what our pediatrician suspected was whooping cough. As her lungs filled with fluid, our pediatrician advised that she needed to be hooked up to a heart monitor unless we were willing to monitor her breathing constantly around the clock. Because our boys agreed to share two-hour shifts throughout the night, we opted to watch her. I never heard one word of complaint as our sons conscientiously took their shifts throughout the night and then went on to school in the morning.

On one of those nights, when it was my shift, our eldest son carried his sleeping bag into the family room we had temporarily set up as our baby's bedroom. Even though I told him I did not need a companion, he insisted. I could see that he wanted to talk. Soon, I figured out what was troubling him. He said, "Mom, if Cam dies, I don't want to be a Christian anymore!"

I was inwardly heartsick hearing such forbidding words from a son I knew loved God very much. I hoped he did not mean what he had said. Still, I tried to comprehend the depth of the emotion he was expressing. Ignoring his actual words, I began to grasp what he was really feeling. "Honey, you love her an awful lot, don't you?" That love was what was making him agonize so.

The depth of a brother's feelings portrays the glue that binds a crossracial adoption, permeating far deeper than the shallowness of physical characteristics. She is *our* child.

Susanna took her crossracially adopted son to a restaurant for lunch. They were noticed by another child and her mother. After their lunch was finished, this curious little girl led her mother by the hand to the table where Susanna and her son sat. Not being able to contain herself a moment longer, the little girl blurted out, "Why don't you look like your Mommy?"

To which the little boy replied, "'Cause she's a girl!" Physical differences obviously were not bothering that little boy.

We will forget that our crossracial children are adopted. The world won't. Let's have grace, humor and pride that adoption was the way God chose to bring a child into our home. As we model these attitudes, others will notice—and we will affect the world, one person at a time

8

ADOPTING THE OLDER CHILD

> At the end of every three years, bring all the tithes
> of that year's produce and store it in your towns,
> so that the Levites (who have no allotment or
> inheritance of their own) and the aliens, the
> fatherless and the widows who live in your towns
> may come and eat and be satisfied, and so that the
> LORD your God may bless you in all the work
> of your hands.
> DEUTERONOMY 14:28-29

MOST PEOPLE PLANNING TO ADOPT ENVISION A NEW BABY cuddled in their arms being rocked to sleep in a comfortable rocking chair in their cheerfully decorated nursery. Often this mental image becomes a reality. Many infants from all over the world are placed in adoptive homes each year. Adoption during infancy is certainly best for the child. It is also best for the family. Why?

"After a child is four, his I.Q. potential is more or less fixed—but between birth and that age his ability to change is astounding." This dramatic conclusion was determined by Benjamin Bloom, a professor of education, and a group of psychologists at the University of Chicago in an in-depth study of children.[1]

Another major study, Harvard University's Preschool Project, directed by Dr. Burton L. White, has pinpointed a critical period of development in children between eight months and eighteen months of age. He concluded that a child's "experiences during these brief months do more to influence future intellectual competence than any time before or after."[2]

The Harvard Preschool Project further emphasized that the single most important factor in the life of a child is his mother. She has more influence than any other person or circumstance. Furthermore, the nuclear family is the most important educational system.

Our overseas staff knows that I feel a great urgency to place babies in their adoptive homes as young as possible. Together we work very hard to efficiently prepare necessary paperwork so that babies can come home to their new families at the earliest possible moment.

Further, these studies confirm that family relationships are crucial to children in helping them develop and learn normally. They validate why I feel such passion about providing homes for children who need parents.

I will persevere in placing the youngest possible babies in families because I know it is in their best interest. But I feel just as passionately that children who did not have the privilege of being placed in adoptive homes as babies still need families to love and nurture them, to give them the best possible chance to grow into the adults God meant for them to be.

Thousands and thousands of adoptable children who were not placed in homes as infants could thrive in families who are willing to open their hearts and homes to love and adopt them. All adoption agencies have lists of waiting children over the age of three. In the United States alone, almost 49,000 adoptable children over the age of one waited for families in 1993 and didn't get them. Yet some of our most successful adoptive placements have been those with older children.

The processing time for these children is usually considerably shorter than for infants, since the number of families waiting for them is considerably less. Sometimes fees are lower in hopes of encouraging families to consider an older child. Still, there is a need for families to approach these adoptions with their eyes wide open. What issues does an adoptive parent of an older child face?

Some older children have younger siblings who by law must be placed together with them. An older child may have a past filled with disappointment, neglect or abuse. Parents who adopt these older children will need to be prepared for their new children to grieve, feel anger and perhaps engage them in a power struggle. Wise parents will give older adopted children plenty of time and space in which to learn to bond.

Can older child adoptions be successful and enriching? When adoptive parents are prepared for the issues involved, the answer is a resounding yes. Let's investigate how.

The Issue of Siblings

Sometimes children available for adoption have brothers or sisters or both. If so, by law the children must be placed as a group. Many of us have heard stories of twins separated at birth who did not know the other existed until some act of God brought them together. Realizing the tragic loss people like these experience—it would be inhumane to separate family members—the law says they must be kept together at all costs.

How does it come about that a sibling group is available for adoption? Often they are true orphans in that both of their parents have died, perhaps in an accident. Other times the children have become wards of the court because their parents' rights have been terminated due to problems like alcoholism or domestic violence. Unlike many individual older children, siblings have not usually spent their entire lives in institutions. At some point the children were most likely living together with their parents as a family—at least until the youngest child was born.

We have had available for adoption sibling groups of two, three and four children. One of the sibling groups we placed was to a childless couple. What a difference the space of a year made in the life of this family! They grew from a childless couple the Christmas before to their first family Christmas picture the next year consisting of Mom, Dad, two brothers, ages five and two, and a one-year-old baby sister, all dressed in snowsuits, smiling in front of three huge snowmen!

Parents considering adopting a family group might benefit from developing a support group of people who can baby-sit or help in an emergency. Parenting an instant family can make it easy for a couple to overlook their own needs in the frenzy of children competing for attention. They may want to protect themselves by making sure they have some time alone.

Although some families may feel they are cutting costs or getting a "Twofer" (two for the price of one) by adopting a sibling group, this is not likely the case. Families need to make sure they have considered the costs carefully before taking a group of children. Couples need to think about agency costs, children's airplane tickets, and the ongoing costs of housing, outfitting and feeding a group of children all coming at once.

Issues of a Child's Past

If an older child has been institutionalized most or all of his or her life, it is likely that the child will have some developmental delays due to lack of stimulation or neglect. Because of inadequate funding in most orphanages around the world, educational toys, equipment and books are often scarce, giving the children little with which to play or interact. With tight budgets even paper and paints or crayons might be an unknown luxury.

Although too much too soon can overwhelm them, families can very slowly introduce their newly adopted older children to new experiences, one at a time, to help make up for the lack of stimulation that an older child has encountered. A family from the Midwest who adopted a three-year-old described his walking around their home for several days with a dazed look on his face, absolutely overwhelmed by all the new things he was seeing, hearing, smelling, tasting and feeling.

Another adoptive mother visited a toy store with her newly adopted four-year-old son in order to buy him a "big-wheels" type of tricycle. His eyes were wide as she wheeled him up and down the aisles of toys in her shopping cart and as she placed the large box containing the tricycle into her cart. Suddenly, on the ride home, the realization that the tricycle was for him penetrated his understanding, and he grabbed his new mother's arm, planting kisses from wrist to shoulder as he repeated, "Thank you, thank you, Momma!" over and over. He simply could not imagine having a bike of his own.

A family counselor advised a family who adopted a five-year-old to think of him as a much younger child until he had a chance to catch up. When we understand that the nuclear family is the single biggest factor in a child's education, we will realize that no one is to be blamed for an institutionalized child's lack of development. Many older children catch up rather quickly once they are with their new families. For others, the process is much slower.

Some children adopted when they are older have been the victims of abuse at some point in their lives. Perhaps the reason their parents' rights were terminated was domestic violence or sexual abuse. Perhaps a stressed or untrained caregiver mistreated a child. We know of an orphanage where caregivers used a swing set as a tool of punishment for the children instead of a toy to be enjoyed. When the children misbehaved they were taken outside and pushed higher and higher on the swing until they screamed to be let down. In another institution we saw children shrinking back, protecting their faces from an orphanage worker who treated them harshly.

By far the majority of caregivers in orphanages around the world work very hard to provide the most loving care possible for the children in their care. Still, there are instances where children have been mistreated or abused, and families adopting older children need to be aware of the possibility. If physical or sexual abuse is suspected, the children may need special counseling to help them overcome their past.

Adjustment of Older International Children

Parents of children who are adopted internationally when they are older explain that the language barrier is not a problem for long. Some families study their child's native language before the adoption in order to prepare for their son or daughter's arrival. Others with little advance preparation utilize a picture dictionary. All, regardless of their language preparation, admit to doing a lot of pointing. And all have agreed that they learned an amazing number of words in their child's native language in the first weeks of being together, as did their child in English. For most the child was doing very well communicating in English within about six weeks of his or her arrival in the United States.

A child will not automatically remember his or her native language. Families who want to help their children remember it must provide opportunities for them to continue to hear and speak it. Sometimes children will refuse to continue to speak their native language after they have learned English. These children are illustrating their intense desire to bond and blend into their new families and culture. Wise parents will not push their children to continue with their native language until a later time when they are interested.

For some children, who have long dreamed of a mother and father and family, traveling to their new life is a dream come true. They may never look back. Some older children, who have lived long enough in an orphanage to have strong memories and attachments there, will grieve the loss of everything familiar to them. Parents who know that grieving is a natural part of a child's transition into a new family will handle this in stride.

One family who adopted a beautiful eight-year-old girl discovered in the first few weeks after their arrival home that everything was better in their daughter's country of birth than it was in the U.S.! No matter what the family said or did, nothing was as good as it had been in the orphanage. This new family lived in the country. Their daughter told them the city where she had lived was far superior. If they rode in their van, riding in a bus was better. When the summer Olympics came, she cheered for her native country, never for the United States.

Yet this same little girl was the one who later came to her adoptive mother and declared, "Momma, thank you, thank you for coming to the orphanage to get me." What was this little girl doing? Was she ungrateful? Not at all. She had to make peace with her loss before she was ready for a new relationship.

Another eight-year-old handled her sense of loss in part by using swear words. For many weeks this child, who had lived her life in an orphanage and now had a terrific new family, called her new father a vulgar name. She fought incessantly with her new sister. It would have been easy for a family to take the anger and evident rejection personally. It would have been easy to jump to the conclusion that this child was ungrateful and to grow angry in return. However, if a family discerns that anger is one way a child responds to loss, they can try to sympathize with their new child instead of allowing that behavior to cause strain between them.

Another adjustment certain families have endured with older-child adoptions is a struggle for power or control. With so many changes occurring in a child's life, he or she may subconsciously feel out of control. Everything is new, including clothes, furniture and surroundings. This child can not communicate clearly in English. He or she does not know what events to expect on any given day because of new routines. And this child does not know the limits and freedoms his or her new mother and father will set. It should not be surprising if the child struggles for control.

I was very clearly a participant in a power struggle several years ago when our staff escorted two little boys to the United States. One afternoon before we left the boys' country, we had several free hours, and so we decided to go shopping. You may be thinking that this idea does not even *sound* sensible, and you are correct. But it seemed rational at the time, and so off we went.

I may never again be quite the same after that shopping escapade. I held each boy by a mittened hand. Dressed in their bulky winter coats and scarves, they looked like darling wooly bears. Their looks won my affection, but their behavior did not. Whenever I tried to lead them in a direction in which they did not want to go, as if on command they would both relax, letting their bodies go totally limp. Then I had two woolly lumps lying on a snowy sidewalk which was filled with disgusted walkers who had to step around them.

In my efforts to get the boys standing, I tried coaxing them, in English of course, which was useless. I lifted their weighty bodies and stood them in a vertical position which seemed effective until I began to walk again. Once more they fell limp on the snow. We repeated the pattern countless times until I was physically and emotionally exhausted. The boys efficiently kept me from shopping. These children are not the only ones who have tested the adults in their lives to see who is in control.

Although most older children bond closely with their parents in time, a few will have trouble trusting their new parents and receiving affection from them if they have never before experienced a close relationship. As we have discussed, a child who is unable to form loving, trusting relationships may have attachment disorder. Spending time with your children and giving them time to bond will help them build trust. They will need plenty of time to get to know you and you them. After all, you may have years for which to make up. If attachment disorder is suspected, a family will benefit from professional counseling to help them deal effectively with this problem.

Adjustment of Older Children Adopted in the U.S.

A mother who adopted three girls, now ages twelve, fourteen and sixteen, out of the foster-care system in the U.S. candidly shared with me her story. Although information regarding their daughters' background is sketchy, it seems that the girls began their journey in and out of foster care when the youngest was two years old.

The girls' biological mother had a history of drinking and drank heavily during at least two of her pregnancies. The father was an alcoholic and was abusive to the mother, and the children showed signs of neglect, including severe malnutrition. The oldest could not read at age nine and the middle daughter could not speak in sentences at age seven. After being shuffled back and forth between home and foster care several times, the girls came to live with their present family as foster children. Although this foster mother was acquainted with neglected children, having worked with emotionally disturbed children who were wards of the state, she said that she and her husband found the transition from being a couple without children to being the parents of three troubled siblings to be difficult.

She explained that just sorting through the children's needs and handling a five-, seven- and nine-year-old at the same time was nearly overwhelming. Their adjustment has involved working through learning disabilities, probable effects of alcohol consumption during pregnancy (fetal alcohol syndrome), speech therapy, anger, sexual abuse and attachment disorder. The foster parents adopted the girls nearly four years after they came to live with them.

Has there been progress? The mother explained that the two older girls are doing well, though the youngest still struggles with attachment disorder. Recently the oldest gave a tribute to her adoptive mother on Mother's Day. This teenager declared publicly that she is grateful for her home and appreciates her family because she is old enough to remember what her life was like before she came to them.

What kind of family can weather the challenges of adopting older children out of foster care in the U.S.? Families like this one who are determined to do whatever is needed to help their children grow and function. Families who are willing to abandon traditional stereotypes of what constitutes a family and realize that their family may be different than others. Families who will take steps to make sure they as parents get adequate time for their own physical, emotional and spiritual nourishment, so that they do not burn out as day in, day out challenges are presented to them. Families who make use of a support system of family, friends and professionals who will become a team to offer assistance as needs arise. And most important, families who realize that on their own they are *not* adequate to meet all of a child's needs. They further understand that God is the one who made these children, and he understands what they have gone through. He can give parents wisdom and strength as they seek his guidance. Families who fit this description are desperately needed to love and nurture children in foster care.

Joys of Adopting Older Children

Sometimes parents adopting older children are disappointed that they missed their children's infancy and early childhood. They don't know when their children got their first teeth, took their first steps or spoke their first words. These "firsts" are all part of the bonding that occurs between parents and their children, making them a family.

Celebrating "firsts" for an older child adopted into a family can help them bond together with their families in the same way. As one mother who adopted a two-year-old said, "I didn't get to see my child take her first steps. So we celebrated the first time she learned to skip!" Looking for milestones you can celebrate together is a concrete way to help an older child bond to you his parents. With creativity, any "first" can be cause for celebration and bonding together.

One of my most memorable trips to the airport took place last year. Two years before, our staff had escorted a seven-year-old girl named Olga home to her new parents in the United States. With much patience, love and prayer from her new family and the support of family and friends, Olga blossomed into a healthy, radiant little girl. With the same love and concern that her parents had for her when they introduced her to music and swim lessons, they introduced her to God, who loved them all so much that he brought them together across an ocean to be a family.

Every night in her bedtime prayers Olga prayed for her best friend, Svetlana, whom she had left behind in the orphanage. As time passed, Olga began praying that perhaps Svetlana could become her sister. The family finally called us, and we were able to confirm that Svetlana, too, was an adoptable child.

Imagine our joy when the airplane landed and Olga stood at the gate, arms outstretched, waiting for Svetlana to get off the plane. One with shiny dark hair, the other with flaxen curls: because of an eight-year-old's prayers, two best friends became two sisters. Older children deserve families just as much as babies. Can adoption of an older child be successful? Ask Olga.

9

THE ISSUES OF INTERCOUNTRY ADOPTION

"Do not deprive the alien or fatherless of justice."
DEUTERONOMY 24:17

THROUGH THE YEARS MY OWN CHILDREN HAVE GRACIOUSLY given me permission to travel to other countries so that I can help other children who do not have moms and dads. They have seen pictures and videos of orphanages as well as being the recipients of trinkets, children's books and local currency from each of the countries I have visited. Sometimes they pray for orphan children or hold helium-filled red, white and blue balloons at the airport gate in anticipation of a family's arrival with their new child from overseas.

Still, I have never been sure how my children have processed all the visual data they have witnessed. Sometimes I wonder how much of my work they really understand. Recently I got a glimpse of how the passion I carry for orphans around the world had affected one of my biological children when he probed, "Mom, when I'm older will you show me pictures of when I was in the orphanage?"

While to this child it may seem like everyone is adopted, the truth is that very few orphan children in the world ever receive the gift of an adoptive mom or dad. The number who are is merely a drop in a bucket compared to the number who face life without parents and little hope for the future. Every country in the world has children who need parents. Who will love these children? Who will give them the opportunities they deserve in order to grow up into healthy, productive adults?

As we have seen in chapter eight, studies confirm that parents are the single most important educational tool for a child. What, then, is to become of children who have no parents? What will happen to those children who have no choice but to spend their childhoods in an institution? Will they develop normally? Will they learn to love and trust other people? Will they learn the lessons we take for granted growing up in a family?

A child growing up in an orphanage is a child at risk. Blame is not to be placed on orphanage caregivers who often give tirelessly, trying to stretch their own reserve of love to all the children in their care. I heard one orphanage director announce with pride that his son was going to marry one of the girls who grew up in his orphanage.

I know another orphanage director who works incessantly to make conditions better in his orphanage by taking the time to befriend small businesses and courageously challenging them to sponsor projects in his orphanage. He has been able to provide cross-country ski equipment for the children to use, as well as other athletic equipment and musical instruments, through his innovative sponsorship idea.

Many officials and caregivers genuinely love the orphans in their care. Despite the lack of funding or supplies, these people are doing their best to help these children who need parents. I have received beautiful examples of lace work, delicately painted folk art and sewing made by children living in orphanages. I have listened to children living in orphanages sing for me and dance beautiful ethnic folk dances in ethnic dress. I have heard piano pieces played with great feeling and difficult solos played on musical instruments borrowed from teachers in the community who volunteer their time to teach in the orphanages.[4]

But these examples are the exception, not the norm in orphanage conditions. For every person who labors with tireless devotion in orphanage work, there are others who burn out because of the overwhelming responsibility. More orphanages are confronted with minimal food, equipment, supplies and caregivers.

I have visited an orphanage many times that has no running water or plumbing. A shower there is a bucket of cold water pumped outside the orphanage complex and poured over the head of a child while he or she stands on a small concrete pad. On the same concrete slab, the cook rinses and chops her vegetables in preparation for dinner.

An orphanage many miles and countries away from the first has one indoor shower for 350 children. The cook for this crowd has a kitchen with only two knives. It does not take a creative mind to visualize the stark contrast between this kitchen and our own. Yet this kitchen is responsible to feed maybe seventy times as many as most of our families.

Because money is often insufficient, many children in orphanages are fed only *once* per day. In other places there are not enough clothes for everyone to be fully dressed. In a certain orphanage, conditions were so poor that shoes were scarce. Consequently, shoes were rarely worn, and when they were, they seemed to be worn only by selected, favored children. At least that is the perception of a little girl who used to live in that orphanage. Since she was never selected to wear shoes, she began to think she was not worth as much as the children who were.

As you can imagine, when that little girl was adopted she could barely stand to take off her shoes. She would put them on in the morning and remove them the last thing before going to bed. Accordingly, her wise mother searched garage sales to find shoes to help her daughter understand just how valuable she was. A closet full of shoes was a concrete reminder of her value.

A family can teach us certain things in life that no one else can teach us. In fact, no matter how good conditions in an orphanage become, they simply cannot substitute for loving parents when it is possible to provide such. Experience, common sense, studies and Scripture reveal that a nuclear family, consisting of parents and children, is the best way for a child to grow and to be nurtured.

✦Despite the efforts of the best-intentioned people, many children growing up in institutions will be at risk physically, intellectually, emotionally and spiritually. The best chance these children have to grow up as normal, healthy adults is for them to be adopted. We can support humanitarian efforts to raise the quality of health care and orphanage conditions, but nothing will compare with giving these children families to love and nurture them.

The first child we had the privilege of placing from one of the countries of the former Soviet Union was a three-year-old girl, born with a congenital deformity of her hip and leg. The authorities explained to us that if she stayed in her orphanage there would be no possibility of providing the costly medical care and prosthesis she needed. She was at risk physically. "Do you have a family to adopt her?" they wanted to know.

I explained that we were committed to all children, disabled and healthy, and that I would find a home for her. I also clarified that I needed a very special family to adopt this little girl, one who would be sensitive to her specific needs. When I arrived home in the States with only a color photo of the back side of this little blond girl, I wondered whom God would provide to love her.

Within a few weeks of our staff's initial prayers, three families expressed a desire to adopt her. Imagine the delight of us all, on both sides of the ocean, when we located her family. The little girl who needed a prosthesis on her leg was adopted by a mother who wears a prosthesis on her arm!

I witnessed an orphanage director's plea for an orphan child to attend the university because she was such a good student. This child received a rare privilege. For most children in orphanages around the world, a university education is not a possibility. Rarely is there opportunity for them to develop to their full intellectual potential. Life in an institution puts children at risk intellectually.

In most countries children are not permitted to live in orphanages after they are fifteen, sixteen or seventeen years old. They may be turned out on the street with no home and no job. Unless they have been taught specific skills while still in the orphanage, they face a lifetime of menial jobs. Street sweeping or unskilled factory jobs may be an option. Prostitution, drug-dealing and the mafia are also sad but real alternatives.

One of our sons pored over college information in the career center of his high school, dreaming of college campuses and opportunities. Although as one of seven children his possibilities, practically speaking, were not limitless, still he dared to dream because his tennis proficiency gave him scholarship-bargaining ability.

What a milestone our family experienced on high-school graduation night with its parties and celebrations. We virtually catapulted this son into his future. I am confident that he and his friends felt invincible as they anticipated universities and limitless career opportunities. In contrast, a young adult who has grown up in an orphanage and leaves it with few skills and no money will have a hard time feeling self-respect. There will be little to dream about and less to which to look forward.

It will be nearly impossible for these children to feel good about themselves when they face little more than a future of destitution. Sadly, these children are at risk emotionally; yet they, just like my own children, deserve to be able to look forward to a bright and optimistic future. Adoption will give these children that chance. Sometimes I look at my darling daughters, adopted internationally from opposite sides of the world, and wonder what their futures would have been if they had lived out their lives in institutions. Economic constraints in each of those countries could have prevented them from reaching their full potential.

Almost exactly one year after our staff escorted four children from Eastern Europe to their new homes, the adoptive families and staff who worked with them had a reunion at a Burger King restaurant with a huge indoor play structure. Just as everyone sat down to eat, the father of the two boys in the group suggested that we share a prayer of thanks for the food. Imagine our surprise when he asked his older son to pray! I could barely keep my eyes closed. I was riveted to his sincere words, spoken clearly and sincerely in perfect English.

This family had told their two new sons the incredible story of how it happened that they became a family. They told their children that the God of the universe who loved them enough to die for them also loved them enough to bring them together as a family across an entire ocean. This boy—one of the ones who went limp in a power struggle with me on the middle of a crowded city sidewalk exactly one year before—had put his trust and confidence in God's Son, Jesus, because he felt God's loving care in his young life. Children who live their lives in institutions often have little chance to learn about God's amazing love for them.

* Children grow best in a family. Families who have enough love in their hearts to open them to an international child and give that child a home and family have a wonderful opportunity to honor God by serving the needs of one of the orphans whom we know he loves very much.

The Process of International Adoption

The process of international adoption is both lengthy and complicated, yet those of us who have achieved it have found it worth the trouble. In order to understand international adoption, it is important to understand that there are three levels of approval a family needs to seek *before* an adoption can be completed. First of all, every family who adopts, regardless of where they live needs to have a certified home study completed on their family, prepared by a person or agency licensed by the state or country in which they live. Second, a family needs to seek approval from the Immigration and Naturalization Service, the INS, if they live in the United States. The INS must verify that they have met all necessary requirements before giving them permission to bring their adopted child from his or her native country home to the United States. Families living outside of the United States need to make sure the regulations of their country are followed. Third, an adoptive family must complete the international paper work fulfilling all necessary adoption regulations for the country from which they are adopting. This is the same for everyone, regardless of where they live.

The Home Study

The first level of approval for an international adoption is completion of a certified home study by a person or agency licensed by the state or country in which the family lives. Each state and country has minimum requirements which vary slightly. The home study preparer will know what these minimum standards are.

In addition, adoption agencies may have certain requirements for families accepted into their program. They may require the following items:

* an application
* autobiographies written by the prospective parents
* some kind of financial verification, including bank statements, employer verification, U.S. federal income tax forms and credit checks
* letters of reference or other documentation of a family's emotional stability, such as the Minnesota Multiphasic Personality Inventory-2 test (MMPI-2)
* birth certificates
* marriage licenses

Orphans Overseas further requires that every family attend a series of pre-adopt classes or listen to the series on audio tape. In these classes we discuss the delays and difficulties of international adoption. Usually an adoption agency will require all necessary documents in a family's file to be completed before they will schedule a social worker to complete the home study.

Sometimes a family feels that the number of questions asked and the amount of paperwork required for a home study are intrusive. They are essentially right. A couple building their family through a pregnancy does not submit to any screening. But if a family recognizes that an agency is required by law to complete the necessary screenings and that all information is completely confidential, that may ease some of their discomfort.

Besides, every home study must meet federal laws regulating international home study requirements, including

* evidence that a family has never been rejected as an adoptive family or been the subject of an unfavorable home study

* written proof that the resident state of the adoptive family has no record of child abuse or criminal abuse

* verification by the person conducting the study that each adult member of the family has the physical, mental and emotional stability to parent an orphan child, and a recommendation in writing that a family meets conditions for approval as an adoptive family. The social worker preparing the home study must document the number of contacts he or she has had with the family, including a necessary home visit seeing in person each member of the family as well as viewing the family's living conditions.

Home studies completed in the U.S. for international adoptions are valid for eighteen months. A certified home study must be signed by the social worker, dated and notarized.

INS Approval

For families living in the United States, approval by our own federal government is also a necessary step in international adoption. Without this step, a family could never bring an internationally adopted child home. For families living in other parts of the world, satisfying the adoption requirements set forth by their own country is of parallel importance. Most countries have similar pre-adoption requirements; it is necessary for any prospective adoptive family to check with both their country of residence and country of citizenship, if they are different, to make sure the necessary requirements are met in order to bring the child home. U.S. citizens living overseas can bypass INS approval if they plan to live overseas with the child a minimum of two years before bringing him or her into the States.

Every U.S. embassy in the world has people lined up every day in hopes of qualifying for visas to come to the United States. Many people wait months or even years to secure them. A child adopted overseas is a citizen of the country in which he or she is born. As such, that child would need to wait for a visa just like any other citizen from his or her country. But as an adopted child, that international child receives status as an immediate relative of a U.S. citizen, and thus does not have to wait for entry. The forms a family submits to the Immigration and Naturalization Service are to classify a newly adopted child as an immediate relative.

One kind of form is filed if the paperwork is completed *before* a child has been chosen or assigned to a family. This form is called an I-600A orphan petition to classify an orphan as an immediate relative. If application for INS approval is completed *after* a child has been chosen or assigned to a family, then the family will file a form called an I-600 orphan petition to classify an orphan as an immediate relative.

Forms must be accompanied by copies or originals of

* birth certificates
* marriage licenses and/or divorce decrees or death certificates from former marriages
* death certificates
* two sets of fingerprint forms for each adult family member, completed at designated fingerprint sites, in sealed envelopes
* necessary filing fees

Home studies must also be presented before final approval is given, but may be furnished separately if desired.

While processing time varies somewhat state by state, 60 to 120 days is a typical timetable to receive final approval. When approval is final, the family will receive a statement called an I-171H approval. Before families working with Orphans Over-

seas receive an assignment of a child, they must have I-171H
approval. Usually its arrival is cause for great celebration!
Documents submitted will eventually be sent to the American
embassy in the country where the family will apply for their
child's immigrant visa before returning to the States.

All children adopted through intercountry adoption will
need an immigrant visa in order to become a permanent resident in their new parents' country, regardless of the country
involved. Although standardized forms will vary country to
country, the documents needed to bring a child adopted internationally into the adoptive family's country of residence will
likely be the same. Birth certificates, valid passports, marriage
licenses, and home studies are commonly required documents
everywhere.

More Paperwork
When a family has completed their home study and has
received their INS approval or home-country approval, they
are ready for the assignment of an international child. There
can be some variation of this order. However, most agencies
do not want a child waiting many months for a family to get
their documents in order and will prefer to assign a child after
INS consent is attained.

Agencies vary considerably as to how they assign or select
children. In our agency we will take parameters the family has
set for us within our application form. They may specify the
age, gender, nationality and health of the child.

For children over age two we will often have pictures. For
babies we may not. We try to tell our families not to bond to
a picture because sometimes a child will become unavailable
due to health concerns or some other difficulty during the
process. Still, it is hard for families to refrain from falling in
love with a piece of paper.

I know. I have done it. In the middle of the night one night we received a phone call waking us from a deep sleep. One of our overseas staff asked us if we would adopt a two-year-old girl. All we knew about her was that she was born to a single mother who was unable to keep her and that she was healthy.

We had been picturing a baby. Still, I thought, if this was the child that God picked out for us, I wanted to be open to it. In the morning, the whole family enthusiastically gave their consent as one by one they woke up and I shared the news with them.

Within hours, we received a faxed picture, which Ron snatched first, declaring her a doll. When I saw the picture I wasn't so sure of his proclamation because it was so fuzzy. All that showed up were two large ink blobs which presumably were her eyes and dark ink where her hair was outlined. Nothing else was discernable. Amazingly, though, within moments, I, too, thought she was adorable. We placed our "daughter's" first picture on our refrigerator for several days until the color photo came; it only endeared her to us more. She really *was* adorable.

I carried her picture around for two weeks, studying it every chance I had. Then, just as quickly as she entered our lives, she was gone. It seems that her mother decided that she could sell her daughter to a baby broker, which she did. I knew I should not bond with a picture, but I did. It's very tempting, but it can cause us unnecessary hurt.

Another family received a picture of the child assigned to them by their child's birth country. But when they traveled overseas to pick up their new child, they were given a different baby. Since the baby was practically the same age as the one of whom they had a picture, they went ahead with the adoption. Imagine their surprise when they visited the

American embassy to obtain their new daughter's immigrant visa and met a couple holding the baby whose picture they had been sent!

Foreign papers vary country to country, and a family's facilitating agency will guide them through the paperwork. Most countries will want duplicate sets of originals, and there is cost in securing them. All countries will want certified copies of originals, which will be permanently kept on file in a government or authorized offices—papers such as birth certificates or marriage licenses. Certified copies of official documents like these must be issued by the office (often the secretary of state's) that keeps the originals on file. These certified copies will be notarized by the issuing office. All other documents must be notarized by a notary licensed in the state in which the document is signed. All overseas paperwork must be notarized. Notaries, among other duties, verify the signature of the signer as a valid one.

In addition to a notary, some countries require other documentation on necessary papers. Each state in the U.S. has an official paper of authentication they can attach to a document which has been notarized in their state, verifying that the notary is a registered notary. There are two kinds of state authentication—apostilles for countries that participated in the Hague Convention and state certification for countries that did not. Although both types of authentication accomplish the same purpose, countries do not use them interchangeably. State officials will need to know the country from which a family is adopting in order to authenticate the documents properly.

In most cases, after state certification is completed, the documents must receive federal seals as well. Federal seals are not necessary for documents that have been authenticated with an apostille. Federal seals verify that the state completing the certification is a valid state in the United States.

How did these differences in the process of authentication come about? Several years ago a group of countries met together to make some agreements regarding international adoption. This meeting, called the Hague Convention, produced a multilateral treaty seeking to insure that the rights of adopted children, birth parents and adoptive parents were all respected in international adoption, as well as to standardize the process among all countries involved. After it is ratified by the U.S., agencies facilitating overseas adoptions will need to be certified by a centralized Hague Convention licensing body in addition to the individual state licensing now required. When the U.S. ratifies the Hague Convention, readoption will no longer be a requirement back in the United States, since all adoptions will be finalized overseas.

One concrete way in which adoptive families may recognize whether or not a country is a participant in the Hague Convention is by what authentication seals are required on foreign paperwork. Countries who participated in the Hague Convention require apostilles on each overseas document—a standardized form generated by the convention to take the place of state certification and federal seals. In addition, specific countries will often require their own official seal of authentication on each paper.

Waiting

After documentation is sent overseas, the process can vary from country to country until an adoption is complete. In Russia, for example, all adoptable children must be placed on a national data base allowing Russians first priority to adopt Russian children. This registry is three months long, and a child's adoption cannot be completed until the required time on the registry is finished. If a Russian family wishes to adopt a specific child, that child will no longer be available to a foreigner.

Sometimes after a child in a foreign country is assigned, officials will require the family to come there to submit their paperwork in person and then to come again later to pick their child up. Although this practice is not widespread, families contemplating international adoption should be aware of the possibility.

Sometimes delays occur. At one point our Asian adoptions were being processed within about four weeks, and families could travel to get their babies when they were about a month old. Because provincial governments have made some changes in their structure of government, processing time is now slower and families may travel when their children are about two months old.

Sometimes extra papers are required or changes occur in foreign adoption laws while a family is waiting for their adoption to be completed. The more flexibility and patience a family can muster in the process of waiting for their child, the better. They will surely need it.

When we first started facilitating overseas adoptions, our staff was able to escort children home from several of the places in which we worked. Laws have changed, and now, for most international adoptions, families must travel to pick their children up. In some countries several families travel as a group; in others one family travels on its own. Our overseas staff hosts our traveling families within the country.

Four of our families traveling together to pick up baby girls encountered discouraging delays overseas. The national government had approved their adoption papers, but the government officials at the local level of government had not. The adoptions were completed, but the local government would not grant the babies their passports. After several weeks of frustrating waiting and much prayer and fasting, the new parents finally had their babies released to them. We think God may have some very special plans for those baby girls as they grow up! Immediately after their release the national government issued a temporary moratorium halting all adoptions while they reorganize their adoption structure.

The Immigrant Visa

After the adoption papers are completed overseas for an international adoption, the family must go to the U.S. embassy that handles immigrant visas for the country from which they are adopting. Usually the embassy is in the country itself. Sometimes, in a newly independent country or a country with whom the U.S. does not have formal relations, the family must travel to the U.S. embassy in a neighboring country to seek an immigrant visa for the child. In this case the child and parents may need transit visas to visit this additional country in their travels to adopt. Each will need a visa issued from the country in which he or she is a citizen, so the child's transit visa will be issued by his or her country of birth.

Although a family is responsible for submitting their own papers to the embassy to obtain their new child's immigrant visa for entry into the United States, most agencies are very familiar with all necessary steps and will guide families throughout the process. Once the child has been legally adopted, the country will issue a passport for the child since he or she is a citizen of that country. Finally the U.S. must give the child an immigrant visa so that he or she can enter this country.

The family will need the following papers at the Embassy:
* proof of their I-171-H approval
* copies of their adoption papers and translations
* the last three years of their federal income tax returns to verify their income

* a contractually binding affidavit of support (Form I-864), substantiating to the consular officers that the child will not become a public financial liability
   * the child's birth certificate and translation
   * the child's relinquishment statements and translation
   * the governments' consent to adopt papers and translation
   * documented proof that the child is a legally adoptable orphan

If the child was abandoned, they will want the child's life record in order to put the pieces of the puzzle together.

Verified statements, such as Who found the child? What did they do next? Who had the authority in that country to declare the child an adoptable orphan? These statements, issued by a person in authority, can declare a child an orphan.

If the child has parents, where are their written statements declaring that they are giving their child up because they are unable to care for him or her?

Or if a child's parents have died, where are the death certificates?

   * the child's sealed official medical report, completed at an embassy-approved clinic
   * verification of the child's immunizations
   * agency verification of pre-adopt requirements
   * the child's passport photos (3)
   * the child's passport
   * application form I-230 from the embassy
   * blue I-600 form from the embassy, signed by both parents

These are all pieces of information the examiners at the embassy will ask an adoptive family. Before going to the embassy, it would be wise for an adoptive family to familiarize themselves with all the English translations of their child's adoption papers so that they can answer knowledgeably at the embassy.

The embassy will also need to validate the legality of the child's adoption papers. They may also want to authenticate costs to make sure that the child was not bought. When the examiner is convinced that the child is an adoptable orphan and that the adoption was a legal one, the family will be granted permission to bring their new child into the United States. This is a milestone of accomplishment! Families usually cry with joy when they are finally finished.

Similar steps need to be taken in other countries when a family of citizens of that country adopts internationally. Documents will have to be taken to that country's embassy to request an immigrant visa for the child.

Readoption and Naturalization

When an adoptive family returns home, several more steps must be taken to complete an international adoption. Although the adoption was a legal one according to the laws of the country from which a child came, still most states in the U.S., and some other countries, require a family to go through what is usually called a *readoption.*

The family's state of residence will usually require the child's birth certificate, adoption papers, "green card" (resident alien card), home study and disclosure of costs—along with a petition written by an attorney on behalf of the adoptive family. The court will issue an adoption decree. Then a new birth certificate can be obtained from the family's state of residence. The new birth certificate will contain the child's new name and will state that he or she was born to the adoptive parents in his or her native country. No mention is made on the birth certificate of the adoption.

When a family receives the child's new birth certificate, they can apply for U.S. citizenship for their child. This does not happen automatically; it must be completed as a separate step.

Children over age seven must attend naturalization classes. We have some very special pictures taken at citizenship ceremonies for internationally adopted children.

When our first baby daughter was escorted off the plane by my husband, we felt our wild roller-coaster ride had finally ended. We felt both thrilled and exhausted. Our second son, David, seeing his baby sister for the first time, blurted out, "Andrea's so beautiful she *needs* five brothers to take care of her!"

Every child living in an institution or orphanage anywhere in the world deserves to hear words of endearment from families who offer that child love. International adoption gives many children that chance. Who will love these children who need parents? Families who adopt them. One child, one family at a time.

10

ISSUES IN DOMESTIC ADOPTION IN THE U.S.

Defend the cause of the weak and fatherless;
maintain the rights of the poor and oppressed,
PSALM 82:3

SEVERAL TIMES DURING MY LIFE I HAVE HELD A SHOPWORN BIT OF paper which symbolizes an event in my infancy that nearly altered the course of my life forever. Knowing I am an adopted child, you may think I am referring to my adoption papers. I am not. This water-stained, smeared fragment is a baby's feeding schedule and a recipe for formula. It looks out of place in a box of special keepsakes, but it's not.

This paper was typed by my adoptive mom the day my birth mother was going to come back for me, having changed her mind about my adoption. My mom dressed me in her favorite dress, and my dad held me one last time and said goodby before leaving for work that morning.

My birth mother had not signed relinquishment papers before my placement with my adoptive family. Still, the social worker felt confident that my birth mother wanted to place me in an adoptive home. For weeks my birth mother agonized over her decision. Could she keep me, or should she let the adoption take place? She worked out the best circumstances she could for my care with relatives and decided she would take me back. It was at this point that my adoptive parents were notified that they would have to say goodby to me, their baby girl.

Trying to keep busy, Mom packed my diaper bag with several bottles for the trip the social worker said I would be taking. All morning she kept trying to force from her mind the inevitable realization that she was losing her baby. Finally she lost her inward battle for control over her emotions, and her tears began to flow, splashing all over the feeding schedule she had typed for my birth mother.

She sat and waited. Her weepy eyes watched the minute hand on the clock racing toward the hour set for my repossession. Suddenly the phone interrupted her aching silence. The message was for the social worker, asking her to call her office when she arrived.

When the social worker pulled in, my mother met her at the door. She gave the phone message to this woman who weeks before had brought her such joy and now such pain. My mother waited while she called, willing the final moment of goodby to be stalled as long as possible.

Not wanting to be impolite, yet sitting within hearing distance, my mother could tell the second call the social worker made was long-distance. My destiny was decided in that long-distance phone call that the social worker made while my mom held me in her arms. It was a call to my birth mother.

She explained to the social worker that she realized now that though she loved me, she had nothing to offer me. She decided that she wanted me to experience the love that both a mother and father could provide. She asked the social worker to tell my parents that I was once again theirs! In an incredibly unselfish act, my birth mother put what she had concluded were my best interests before her own. She signed the relinquishment papers.

This story had a happy ending for my mother and father as adoptive parents. Not all birth parent-adoptive parent tugs-of-war end in joy. Many people live in terror of a birth parent's returning to take their baby away.

For these reasons, domestic adoptions are both cherished and feared. Thoughts of a newborn just hours old, straight from the hospital, still fresh with umbilical cord and newborn smell, fill the hearts of many families seeking adoption. Still, many do not proceed with a domestic adoption because of the fear of interference or disruption by the birth family.

Of what issues should a family be aware who is considering a domestic adoption, and what is involved in the process?

Demand and Supply

In the United States, the demand for Caucasian infants to adopt is very high. Many parents want their adopted children to look as much as possible like their biological children, and those who are childless want the experience of parenting a newborn.

Our own family had the joy of bringing our domestically adopted son home from the hospital when he was less than twenty-four hours old! This privilege would have been impossible in an international adoption. Other families are able to witness their baby's birth or feed their baby his or her first bottle. With hormone supplements, a few adoptive moms even nurse the baby.

Because of the special interest in Caucasian infants, agencies and attorneys who place them for adoption often have waiting lists three and four years in length. Some, taking advantage of the situation, charge significantly higher fees for

Caucasian newborns than for other adoptions. This practice seems to imply that some children are more valuable than others. Most of us who read these pages would passionately protest, confirming our belief that all children in the world are of equal value. Still, the economic principle of supply and demand sometimes applies to adoptions in the same way it does to cars and paintings. A family considering domestic adoption must grapple with these ethical issues. They must ask themselves appropriate questions and make sure that they feel at peace with the answers they find.

And the fact is, for every adoption facilitator who abuses adoption and uses it for personal economic gain, there are many more individuals who work tirelessly on behalf of children because they have a passion for children and because it gives them tremendous satisfaction to see children and families united.

Families will gain insight by asking to see a breakdown of adoption fees and expenses to decide whether or not they are reasonable. Because it is legal in some states to make profit from adoption, fees charged can vary dramatically. A family would be sensible to compare fees and expenses from several agencies or private adoption contacts to find a fee and expense scale with which they feel morally and financially comfortable.

If confronted with a long waiting time for adoption, families need to grapple with another decision. Is it more important to wait indefinitely for the baby of their dreams, or might they have a more fulfilling alternative by adopting a child from somewhere else in the world who needs a family right now? Every family will answer this question differently, since adoption is a personal matter, but the issues should be considered.

Adoption Loss

For the social work community, it is common knowledge that

the greatest percentage of single young women in the United States who carry their pregnancies to term will end up keeping their babies. Most professionals would conservatively estimate that at least 85% of these young women will become single mothers, despite the options they consider during pregnancy.

Many people wonder why so many single young women are delivering babies outside of marriage in our country. Beyond that, we wonder why so many are choosing to keep them and become single parents. Though there is no concrete proof, still trends would suggest a possible cause for this problem which is unique to the United States.

Fifty years ago in our nation, if a teenager became pregnant she was banished from school and perhaps sent away to give birth secretly and place the baby in an adoptive home. Her only alternative was a "shotgun" wedding where she and the father of the baby would quickly marry to legalize the baby they had conceived.

With the legalization of abortion in the United States by 1973 and an increase in the availability of contraception, sexual activity among unmarried young people dramatically increased. The social stigma of sexual activity outside of marriage diminished. Today pregnant teenagers are "supported and embraced in their decision to give birth, keep their babies, continue their education, and participate in school activities."[1]

As we have noted, well over one million births per year in the U.S. are out-of-wedlock births. Some of the babies born to these young women are well cared for, but many are children at risk. Without sufficient vocational skills, these mothers will face minimum-wage jobs, yet have staggering expenses related to child care and costs for their babies. Many live at the poverty level. Lack of emotional support, education and parenting skills can open the door to potential child abuse. No one with high ethical standards would ever pressure a young woman into choosing adoption for her baby. Still, for many of those children born to single mothers, adoption would better meet their needs.

But the overwhelming majority of young women who come to us for counseling during their pregnancies tell us they could never think about placing their babies for adoption. Among the few who seriously consider adoption, many discover that fighting popular opinion is too difficult, so they change their minds and end up keeping their babies.

This reversal can be both an emotional and financial risk to a family. Prospective adoptive parents who have helped a birth mother with living expenses and, if the child is already born, with the cost of the birth, may have a financial loss. More serious is the devastating emotional loss when the birth mother changes her mind and the child they counted on is lost to them.

Maria, a young woman our agency had the privilege of counseling, never ever wavered throughout her pregnancy concerning her plans to place her baby for adoption. She carefully selected her family among several profiles of prospective families and met with them twice to interview them. Together they worked out a semi-open relationship agreeable to them all.

After she delivered her baby, Maria asked for her adoptive family to come to the hospital, which they did. They spent time together in the recovery room and snapped photographs to preserve their baby's first moments. When she signed the adoption papers she burst into tears, and the agency worker realized she was not ready to make the decision. The adoptive parents went home without their baby. A week later Maria confirmed her decision and kept her baby.

Knowing the risk of an adoption loss or reversal in a domestic adoption, many adoptive parents try to keep some emotional distance during the waiting time. Knowing the statistics, I did that too. Even after our family had been chosen by a birth mother, I still did not plan on a baby. I did not take the crib out of the attic, nor did I open my trunk of newborn clothes to get them ready for our new baby. Even after we saw our adorable newborn boy in the hospital nursery and fed him his first bottle, I still was not convinced we would really be his parents. Certainly I wanted him, but I was bracing myself emotionally for a possible disappointment.

Finally our attorney called and said that the birth parents had signed their relinquishment papers and we could meet him at the hospital to take our baby home. At last I decided it was time to unpack the trunk and wash the newborn clothes! Was it necessary to be so cautious? Probably not. But I did not want to be crushed if things didn't work out the way I hoped.

Because of my protective shell, it was difficult for me to immediately turn on those emotions that I had before so effectively repressed. In the first few weeks following our adoption, I loved our baby dearly, but I felt as if I were baby-sitting for someone else's baby. It took almost a month before I felt he was fully mine. Not everyone will find the bonding process a slow one. Families who have guarded their emotions may find it slower than those who have not.

Adoptive parents who are considering domestic adoption need to be aware that a birth mother who chooses them may change her mind before the adoption is completed. They should be prepared to meet that loss if it occurs. If parents would find the loss of a potential adoption too difficult to handle, possibly they should not consider domestic adoption.

Overlooked

Today's birth mother who chooses adoption usually wants to

choose the family for her baby. Agencies do not have the full
responsibility of placement. Sometimes wonderful families are
overlooked by birth mothers.

Families with two or more children may not seem as suitable
to a birth mother as a family who has no children. Older
prospective families may be overlooked in favor of younger
parents. One birth mother I know of discarded a family, after
she had seen their picture profile, because the family's little
child was wearing "moon boots" in the snow. She remarked,
"No child of mine in going to wear moon boots!" She chose
another family to parent her baby. Families who feel uncomfortable relying on a birth mother's selection may want to consider either adopting a child whose parental rights have been
terminated by the state or adopting internationally.

The actual process of a domestic adoption involves much
less paperwork than an international adoption. What does the
process involve?

The Home Study
The home study for a domestic adoption is similar to that for
an international adoption. Each family will need to have a
home study completed in the state in which they live by a person or agency licensed by the state as competent to complete
home studies. The person preparing the home study will seek
to determine if the prospective family meets the minimum
requirements of adoption for that state.

In order to complete the home study an adoption agency
may want to see the following papers:
* the application
* credit checks
* letters of recommendation

They may also require participation in pre-adopt classes.
The social worker, just as in an international home study, will

complete an in-home interview with all family members present. A domestic home study is valid for two years.

Adoptive Family Profile

Another preparatory step for a domestic adoption is a profile prepared for the birth mother. Different agencies have slightly different requirements, but usually a nonidentifying letter to a birth mother is included as well as a picture page. The letter usually highlights the family's interests and the strengths they have to offer a child. The pictures should reveal an engaging glimpse of family life. We encourage families to put their creative personalities into a profile, realizing that the packaging is part of the impression.

I watched a birth mother reject one family in her final choice in part because another file was more attractively put together. Though it seemed the first family was a better fit with the birth mother's hopes for her child, the family had hurriedly scribbled their letter on a spiral notebook page which they had ripped out to send. Their family pictures were still in the photo processing envelope. Although the content of their letter was deep and thoughtful and their pictures delightful, they came in second, in part because of the packaging.

The other family had taken the time to mount the pictures attractively with hand-written captions and a calligraphy border. We who believe in God's sovereignty know that the first family could have been chosen without the frills of packaging, but everything given to a birth mother in a family's profile is part of the impression she receives from that family. It will all play a part in her choice of to whom to delegate the task of parenting her child.

Birth mothers want to *feel* what a prospective family is like. They want to know our passions. This is an excerpt of the letter I wrote to the mother of our son:

As a mom, my highest priority for my children is for them to grow up loving Jesus and being obedient to him. More than anything else, I want to know that someday we will be in heaven together. I believe that one of the best ways for me to help them learn to love Jesus is for me to work on becoming the person God wants me to be. When they know God is important to me, it usually makes them want to know him too. Even though I try hard, I'm not a perfect mom. Sometimes I fail, and then I need to tell my children I'm wrong and ask them to forgive me. But as they see me admitting I'm wrong, they learn to say they are sorry too.

Occasionally a birth mother will request a video as part of the profile as well.

The Selection Process

As we discussed in chapter 5, when a birth mother has selected several families whom she likes, she may decide to have an informal meeting with them, usually one family at a time and on a first-name basis only. If the birth mother is really interested in a specific family, she may discuss the conditions of the relationship she desires with them, including whether or not she wants them to participate in the birth experience and how often she wants to have contact or receive pictures after the baby is born.

Some adoptive families feel very threatened when the birth mother wants to spend time with her baby in the hospital. They worry that she will change her mind when she sees the baby. Although this can happen, a mother who chooses adoption for her child will heal faster if she has had sufficient time for closure with her child. Families are wise to support the birth mother in this decision, out of love and concern for her welfare, if she chooses to do so.

If the birth mother wishes an "entrustment" ceremony, a

special planned time of celebration together, marking closure for her and beginning for the new family relationship, she may also discuss this desire with the family. Most often families will draw up an informal contract to confirm their agreement together.

Even if an adoption contract is not legally binding in the state in which you live, it is an important link between a birth mother and her child—a link she will count on for many years to come. In a domestic adoption the adoptive family receives a child, whereas a birth mother receives a promise. Thoughtful families will take great care to honor their contracts out of respect for the mother of their child.

Legalization

While in most states birth fathers can sign relinquishment papers anytime before the baby is born, the birth mother must always sign after the baby is delivered. Some states regulate how soon a birth mother can sign. Other states will not allow a birth mother to sign while she is still in the hospital. Laws dictating the amount of time birth parents have in which to surrender their babies and how much time they have to change their minds after they have surrendered vary considerably state to state. Laws apply in the state in which the mother gives birth even if she lives somewhere else. "Laws can be more liberal for birth parents, such as in the state of Pennsylvania. There, birth parents have seventy-two hours to surrender and another forty-five days to decide to revoke the surrender. At the other end of the spectrum, more favorable to adoptive parents, is Missouri where birth parents sign irrevocable surrenders in forty-eight hours."[2] Other states may fall somewhere in between.

In order to give themselves the best chance to have an uncontested adoption, the adoptive family needs to be aware of adoption laws in the state in which they live and also, if the two are not the same, in the state in which the birth occurs. If two states are involved, the Interstate Compact (which must be carefully adhered to) will regulate the cooperation between the states. Agencies or adoption attorneys will know these regulations; families who are concerned about the welfare of their adoption must take the time to become knowledgeable as well.

A domestic adoption with the most security from possible disruption will be the one where both birth parents have signed the relinquishment papers giving permission to place their baby for adoption. Sometimes this is not possible, and then a family must decide if they are willing to face the risks involved. The birth mother's signature alone is not enough to make her child available for adoption. Sometimes the birth father is not available to sign the papers. Sometimes the birth father is unknown. These factors complicate the adoption process and increase the risk.

It is important for the adoptive family to understand their state's definition of "father" when considering the birth father's relinquishment. If a birth mother is married, her husband is considered the child's legal father even if he is not the biological father. Then there is the biological father, whether he is involved or not.

In addition, there may be a "putative," or supposed, father when the birth mother is not sure who the father of her baby is. Possibly there are several putative fathers. The rights of all possible "fathers" need to be terminated in order for an adoption to be without risk. First the father or fathers need to be identified. Then they must be given a chance to sign surrenders voluntarily. If a father is unwilling to sign or is unavailable, it is possible to terminate his rights without surrender, but this is a costly and difficult process, necessitating a court hearing to prove that the father is an unfit parent.[3] Many families do not wish to become embroiled in such an expensive and exhausting process. Each family should consider their ability to live with potential risks in an adoption without proper surrenders.

An adoption agency or attorney will have the adoptive parents sign the necessary legal papers after the birth parents have completed theirs. The adoptive parents will need an attorney to submit their adoption papers to the court. A social worker will monitor the family's progress until the adoption is finalized; the timing varies state to state. Adoption finalizations are celebrated in many ways. Sometimes the family appears in court personally; sometimes the papers are sent in the mail.

The "Family Circus" comic strip once ran a cartoon featuring adoption. The children are pointing across the street at a neighbor who is pushing her baby in a stroller. The big sister explains knowingly to her brother, "We came from Mommy's tummy. But Joseph is adopted, so he came from his mommy's heart."[4] Domestic adoption is about both tummies and hearts. Both are necessary. Birth parents and adoptive parents need great respect for one another in order for a domestic adoption to be successful.

11

PARENTING THE ADOPTED CHILD

Praise be to the God and Father of our Lord Jesus Christ,
who has blessed us in the heavenly realms with every
spiritual blessing in Christ. For he chose us in him
before the creation of the world to be holy and
blameless in his sight. In love he predestined us to be
adopted as his sons through Jesus Christ, in accordance
with his pleasure and will—to the praise of his
glorious grace, which he has freely given us in the
One he loves. In him we have redemption through his
blood, the forgiveness of sins, in accordance with the
riches of God's grace that he lavished on us with all
wisdom and understanding.
EPHESIANS 1:3-5

THERE IS LITTLE ARGUMENT WITH THE STATEMENT "CHILDREN DO
what those around them do." It is simply a principle of life that
permeates every language and every culture around the
world. Our family is no exception.

Not many people are shocked when I tell them that our family of nine doesn't receive many dinner invitations to other families' homes. Oh, we used to do a lot of entertaining when we were just a couple. Ron and I asked friends into our home nearly every weekend, and often those friends reciprocated. However, we noticed a distinct decline in invitations, directly corresponding to the number of individuals in our growing family.

One unsuspecting family summoned the whole jury. Riding in our van to their home, I felt compelled to give our children a refresher course in manners lest we all be humiliated. Ron must have felt jittery too, because the whole time I was lecturing, he was also giving instructions. Keep in mind that I was not finishing manners. I was framing the shell.

"Don't say 'yuck' if you don't like what is served," I pleaded. "And don't wad up food in your napkin and stuff it into your milk glass." The moment the car ride ended, the kids leaped out of the van.

Amazingly, the evening passed without any headline stories, and soon it was time to go. Too late I realized I had forgotten to remind the children to be sure to thank our hosts. Having missed the deadline, there was nothing to do but watch.

Twelve-year-old Tad started the parade. He shook hands with our hosts and walked out the door, waving over his shoulder, calling, "Goodby, and thank you for inviting us." I was both surprised and delighted with his politeness.

Ten-year-old David followed, also shaking our hosts' hands, walking out the door, waving over his shoulder and calling, "Goodby, and thank you for inviting us."

Beginning to identify a pattern, I was riveted to our seven-year-old son, curious to see what would happen. Luke did not disappoint me, for he shook hands with our hosts, walked out the door waving the same parade wave over his shoulder and called out, "Goodby, and thank you for inviting us!"

Now it was the four-year-old's turn. His performance was by now as predictable as pimples on prom night. Bursting with four-year-old passion, Joel shook the hands of our hosts, skipped out the door, waved his arm over his shoulder faster and faster, like a windshield wiper, and called out at the top of his lungs, "Goodby, and thank you for biting us!"

Children do what others around them do—not because of any conscious thought process or understanding, but simply because modeling is a principle of life and a great means of learning. It is an effective tool adoptive parents can use in parenting their children.

The question most prospective adoptive parents really want to know is, "How can we give our adopted children healthy self-esteem?" I would like to suggest that the key to how an adopted child accepts his own identity as an adopted child will depend greatly on how you, his parents, accept it. You will model the game rules for your adopted children. They will take their cues from you.

When to Tell a Child About Adoption

Numerous parents wonder when is the "right" time to tell a child about his or her adoption. Children will vary in how naturally they talk about their adoptions. Some will incessantly ask questions. Others will recoil at the topic. Experience has shown that parents who begin discussing their children's adoptions at once help them grow comfortable with the topic.

I can remember being bounced up and down on my dad's lap when I was a tiny little girl. He would always ask the identical question, which became a fun ritual for us: "What would I do if I didn't have a little girl like you?"

And I would always return the same answer: "You'd come and find me, Daddy!" I may not have been able to articulate what adoption was, but I knew it was very special. I knew I was very much loved.

With our own children we have done the same. Even while on the changing table I have acknowledged to my babies, "Didn't Jesus love us an awful lot to bring us together across so many miles!" or "You needed a mommy and daddy and we needed a little girl!" They don't have to understand the legal issues of adoption to know that Mom and Dad think it is amazing. And because modeling is a principle of life that is always in effect whether we realize it or not, if we as moms and dads think adoption is extraordinary, our adopted kids will grow up feeling adoption is awesome too.

What will we tell our children about adoption? All parents have the honor of telling their children the *miracle* of the story of how it came to be that they became a family. The story needs no exaggeration or embellishment, just the truth. Everyone has a story. I do. You do. Each child in our family has a different story. Our birth children love to hear their own delivery stories, and they are all unique. And our adopted kids have special stories of their own.

My first labor was one hour and fifty-five minutes from start to finish. As a child, our oldest loved to hear about all the excitement he caused in the delivery room because of such a quick entry. As if living out a legacy, this son has lived on speed-dial ever since. His soccer coach appropriately called him "Jet." Nonetheless his story is an outpouring of God's grace to us, and part of the identity he holds today was formed by understanding the miracle of his own life.

Another son loved the part in his story about my obstetrician driving me to the hospital from our home because he was afraid I would have the baby on the freeway. This boy delighted to hear (over and over again) that the nurses, seeing this doctor bringing a very pregnant patient into the hospital himself, teased him, asking if he had so few patients that he had to find pregnant women on the street!

Another son finds it amazing that I had to endure a C-section without anesthesia for him. Numerous adoptive families have endured much more pain than that in their adoption stories. The history and the pain are all part of the marvel of bringing an adoptive family together. Your child needs to become aware of this miracle. Adopted children's stories are no *less* of a wonder than the wonder of birth. In fact, the miraculous stories of adoption are often *more* incredible.

Families who have both birth children and adopted children will be able to emphasize both the uniqueness of each member of their family and the fact that they were definitely intended to become a family together by understanding how God brought each of them together. Feelings of competition or inferiority diminish when our children understand how special they each are and that each was clearly brought into this family—to love and take care of each other.

What if the circumstances of a child's background are cruel? What if a child was abandoned or deserted? What can we then report to our children? Once again we need to explain the truth to them. I would never encourage a parent to lie to his child. If we do, we will have difficulty teaching our children to trust others, including us.

Nor would I devastate a child by asserting, "Your parents didn't love you!" The same movie can be made for a "G" rating, appropriate for children, or an "R" rating, depending on what is emphasized. Although it would not be ethical to change our children's stories, we have a responsibility to tell the stories in a way that will respect children's ages and dignity.

Despite the conditions of our children's backgrounds, we can learn to emphasize the positive. In a world where abortion is an option available to most women, *all* adopted children can be told that their mothers chose to give them the gift of life, perhaps at great hardship to themselves. Even if she was able to provide nothing more than this, still the favor to you and your child is astonishing.

Even the child who was deserted in a train station can be

told genuinely, "Your parents wanted better for you than they could provide." The same can be said to the child whose mother delivered him or her and ran away from a maternity hospital without any means of identification. These parents would not have left their children where they could be found by someone else if they had not wanted better for them than they could provide.

Further, every adopted child, no matter how desolate the background, can concentrate on the family that was built through the circumstances of his or her adoption. Every family can emphasize the miracle of their child's being found.

Adoption Vocabulary

Whereas to certain people it may seem trivial to mention adoption vocabulary, it too contributes to children's views of themselves as adopted people. *Adoption* is not a negative choice; it is a parenting plan. Birth parents who choose adoption are choosing a plan for parenting their children. Children are *placed* in an adoptive home, not given up for adoption.

Adopted children have two sets of parents; *birth* or *biological parents* and *parents*. If adoptive parents become comfortable in establishing these definitions, their children will become comfortable too. By calling the biological parents birth parents, it allows the adoptive parents to call themselves the parents without always attaching the adjective *adoptive,* as if an apology. You are the parents of your child. In addition, your child has birth parents.

Sometimes adoptive parents unthinkingly call their children's birth parents their "real" parents. If a birth parent is called the "real" parent, is an adoptive parent referred to as the "unreal" parent? Further, a family's biological children are birth children, not "real" children.

Families who have both biological and adopted children are

a *family*. When such a family is introducing themselves, for the sake of the children, who need to blend, it is important to drop all adjectives of explanation. I know of an adoptive mother who felt sad every time her mother-in-law introduced all the grandchildren, because she would introduce her biological grandchildren as "my grandchildren" and this woman's children as "my adopted grandchildren." In like manner, when a parent who has adopted children only introduces them, they should be introduced as your children—which they are! Remembering that our children are always modeling our attitudes and our words will help us use vocabulary thoughtfully.

Roots of Healthy Self-Esteem

These matters of timing, vocabulary and so on are tools that can help our children begin to feel good about themselves, but they are really a very small part of our privilege and responsibility as parents in giving them the gift of healthy self-esteem. Most of us would admit that we have a tremendous desire to be perfect, balanced parents of our adopted children, and as such, we will try our very best.

But what happens when without warning your child suddenly says, "I hate being Asian!" or "Why don't I have blue eyes?" How are you going to respond when your beloved child comes home crying? In between sobs you piece together the story that at recess another child taunted him accusing, "Nobody wanted you!" or, as someone actually once voiced to me, "You should have been an abortion!" How can we brace our children to handle the hurt of living in an insensitive world without its crushing them?

We are not living in a perfect world. Despite our best efforts as parents, we cannot protect any of our children from all the pain of cruel people. Some will do and say hurtful things to them. A few will have prejudiced attitudes toward our adopted children. We cannot control the attitudes, words or actions of other people.

I vowed when we adopted our daughter out of an orphanage that I would never use any part of her background to hurt her. Yet, one day in a moment of frustration, I (who, of all people, should know better) threatened, "Maybe I should send you back to the orphanage!"

Of course I was sorry for those irrational words. Of course I told my little girl that I didn't mean what I had said. But the words *had* been said, and the hurt penetrated. And this is reality. Even parents who love their children very, very much will do and say hurtful things, because no matter how hard we try, we can't be perfect—we are far from perfect. Unless our children's self-esteem is based on something other than being able to perform in an acceptable way, we have no chance of giving them healthy self-esteem.

To what can we turn for a solid basis of self-esteem? Turning to the Bible gives us the answers we need. In Scripture we see clearly illustrated that self-esteem is not dependent on a person's performance or the performance of other people. Our children's self-esteem is dependent on who they are. Who are they? In 2 Corinthians 3:4-5 we are told, "Such confidence as this is ours through Christ before God. Not that we are competent in ourselves to claim anything for ourselves, but our competence comes from God."

Healthy self-esteem is rooted in who we are in relationship to God. He is the one who gives all of us value. Rather than our value in life coming from the things that we do or say, or from the things we do not do or say, it comes from belonging to and being treasured by the God of the universe. We as parents need this truth just as much as our children do.

The moment may come when the child for whom we

longed shrieks, in a moment of disappointment, "You're not my real mom! She would treat me better than you do!" Fewer words spoken to an adoptive parent could cut more deeply than these. If our own identity, our personal sense of value, is rooted in our performance as an adoptive parent, these words from our child's lips will proclaim our utter defeat as a parent.

However, if our personal value is rooted not in our performance as parents but in the value that God has given to us, we can endure crushing words and survive, not needing to take them as personal failure. How does God give us value? In Galatians 4:4-7 we see a picture of that value:

But when the fullness of time had come, God sent his Son, born of a woman, born under the law, in order to redeem those who were under the law, so that we might receive adoption as children. And because you are children, God has sent the Spirit of his Son into our hearts, crying, "Abba! Father!" So you are no longer a slave but a child, and if a child then also an heir, through God. (NRSV)

When we comprehend that God, who created the universe, loved us enough that he sent his only Son, Jesus, to live on earth and to die for us, that understanding gives us unbelievable worth. The Bible further tells us that God longs to *adopt* us as his children.[1] It is an unimaginable gift to realize that God longs to get to know us and longs to tell us we are special.

Those of us who experience the yearning only an adoptive parent can feel while waiting to adopt a child can understand the metaphor the Bible uses to describe God's longing toward each of us. He longs to adopt each of us as his children, desiring the same closeness with each of us as a child has with a parent whom he calls "Daddy" instead of "Father." When we have given our children the understanding of these truths, we are giving them the most important gift we can ever give.

Healthy self-esteem is rooted in comprehending the value God has bestowed on us.

One day one of my children clamored from the back seat, "Mommy, why did Jesus give us a donut?"

I wondered if this child was hungry and trying to get my attention in a creative way, but he wasn't. He really wanted to know. I tried to imagine where he had become confused in his thinking. He had heard it in a song, he persisted. We reversed the cassette tape that had been playing and finally heard the word: "He has given us *atonement* for our sins." To a little boy the words sounded the same.

"Honey," I responded, "Jesus has given us a lot more than a donut."

When Jesus has given us atonement for our sins and has adopted us as his children, the Bible promises us that we become heirs of God. A child or heir of a king is a prince or a princess. When our boys were little, every day before school we would pray that they would remember who they were— that they were princes. If a child was unkind to them on the playground, they could handle the affront better, realizing that they were princes, no matter what anyone said about them. All children need to understand the depth of their value to God. When they have this certainty, it doesn't matter what anyone says or does to them, because they know that they are princes and princesses to God.

When I was a little girl, my mother quoted to me some words that helped me understand that my self-esteem is in God who created me.

When Jesus sent you to us,
We loved you from the start;
You were just a bit of sunshine
From heaven to our hearts.
Not just another baby

'Cause since the world began,
There's been something very special
For you in His plan.

That's why He made you special;
You're the only one of your kind.
God gave you a body
And a bright healthy mind.
He had a special purpose
That He wanted you to find,
So He made you something special;
You're the only one of your kind.[2]

As you help your children understand their incredible value to God, they will have no trouble accepting their identity as an adopted child. Adopted? So are we.

12

NOW WHAT?

"They have become rich and powerful and have
grown fat and sleek. Their evil deeds have no limit;
they do not plead the case of the fatherless to win it,
they do not defend the rights of the poor. Should I
not punish them for this?" declares the LORD. "Should
I not avenge myself on such a nation as this?"
JEREMIAH 5:27-29

ABOUT SIX TIMES PER YEAR OUR AGENCY OFFERS PRE-ADOPT
classes for families interested in investigating the process of
adoption. A few of the families who attend have determined
from the start that they want to adopt and are anxious to begin
the process. Others are barely getting their feet wet regarding
the whole process, and they come to explore the territory.

One such family showed up in our class one morning several years ago, having seen a small announcement in our
church bulletin about international adoption. They were not
infertile. Having birthed three young children of their own,
they were not looking to adoption as a means of expanding
their family. They were not yearning for a child of the opposite gender; they already had two boys and a girl. They simply were drawn to the announcement and wondered if they
might help or be involved in some way.

Today this terrific family has four children. The latest arrival is Hannah, a lovely Asian child. What happened to move a contented family of five to an enriched family of six? As they listened to stories about children in the world who need parents, they grappled with all of the issues presented. They came with an open heart, exploring how God wanted them to be involved, and he gave them a daughter.

What process occurred in their hearts to make them desire an internationally adopted child? For one thing, they had considerable experience with exchange students, so they knew how enriching international relationships can be.

But they grappled with providing financially for yet another child. The husband, especially, pondered the responsibility of future education costs and the reality that more family members meant less to share with each one. He weighed these costs against the intangible riches a new child could bring to them all. This couple wanted to be fair to their birth children. Yet they felt that what the family would receive from this experience far outweighed the financial concerns. In the dad's own words, "How could we *not* do it?"

Further, their faith in God was being stretched. The wife was particularly moved as she heard illustrations of God's having a bigger perspective in mind than we are able to see. She considered her fears of bringing a child with many unknown variables into her already happy, settled family. She weighed these fears against her ability to trust God with those fears and to allow God to choose for them a child that he knew would flourish in their family. She wanted to do the right thing for her family. She confirmed that her faith in God stretched far enough to outweigh her fears. She concluded, "God has blessed us. What better way to celebrate than to share our family with another child!"

Was the process an easy one once they decided to adopt?

You may think so, since they were generously giving of themselves to help a needy child. But it was not easy. Not easy at all. Since their family did not fit exactly into the parameters of the adoption laws in the country they selected, they experienced many delays. They waited several months for a child to be assigned by their selected country and then many more months for approval to travel to pick her up. Throughout the process they prayed about the adoption with their children. Although they did not need to seek their children's permission, they wanted their adoption to be a family experience, and they wanted their children to share in every aspect of it. They named their baby early in the process, so that the children would be able to picture more concretely that they had a little sister who was living in another country.

When Hannah was first assigned to them, they prayed that they would be able to go immediately to get her. After all, they were ready. They were anxious, and waiting was difficult. Their prayers, they confessed, were focused on themselves and on their desire to make things happen *right now*. Then they changed their prayer. They began to focus on Hannah when they prayed. They concentrated on praying that her needs would be met. They felt assured that she was being well cared for, knowing that God was watching out for her. Then they were able to relax, realizing she would come home at just the right time. Taking the focus off of themselves changed their outlook.

Though assigned to them when she was seven months old, Hannah reached the one-year mark while they waited, confident that God wanted her in their home. But still they did not get approval to travel and claim her.

Many families would have been frantic with grief over missing their child's first birthday, but this family chose instead to celebrate. They had a birthday party for Hannah. They wrapped packages, blew up balloons, fixed party food and did everything else expected at a family birthday party. In fact, the only missing ingredient was Hannah! Imagine the story they can tell and the pictures they can show her someday of her first birthday party—all without her. They can show her a concrete example of their trust in God and their commitment and love to her.

Several months later, they finally traveled to bring Hannah home. Things still did not go smoothly, but with perseverance and prayer the family of six is now at home together. Was their adoption worth the trouble, pain and cost? They think so. God thinks so. Their ten-year-old daughter's assessment? "We got the best baby in Asia!"

What happens when we, like this family, are confronted with the knowledge that there are countless children in the world who need families? We, too, need to make a decision of how we will respond.

An Impossible Opportunity?

Since 1986 families from the United States have averaged nearly 9,000 international adoptions per year. An additional five to ten thousand children are adopted worldwide. Considering a recent phone call I had regarding over 1,000 adoptable children from a small geographic corner of the world, the total number of children around the world who need homes right now is far greater than the availability of families ready to take them. There is tremendous hope for the infertile couple who longs to be parents. Even as you read these words, there are children who are waiting for homes. And there are many more children than infertile families and families who are presently waiting for children could even begin to adopt.

Every family needs to carefully consider adoption of a child who needs a home. If you're thinking, "No, we couldn't possibly," arguing that adoption costs are expensive, you are right. But as one of our staff always reminds our prospective families, adoption costs far less than a car! One of my favorite quotes—claimed by several people but the original source unknown—declares, "One hundred years from now it will not matter what kind of house I live in, what my bank account totals or the kind of car I drive. But the world may be different because I was important in the life of a child."

All of us seem to afford those things which are most important to us by making necessary financial choices. In 1996 President Clinton signed an act providing income-tax credits for specified adoption expenses as an incentive to encourage both international and domestic adoptions. Credits of up to $5,000 for healthy children and up to $6,000 for special needs children are possible for families with annual adjusted gross incomes of under $75,000, and partial tax credits are possible for families with adjusted gross incomes between $75,000 and $115,000. Families with annual adjusted gross incomes of over $115,000 are ineligible.

If a family's taxes are less than the adoption expenses, the difference can be deducted more than one year, up to five years maximum. Exemptions apply to the year in which the adoption is finalized. This tax benefit for adoption is a temporary one, good for five years only unless it is renewed. This incentive may provide significant financial encouragement to U.S. families considering adoption, but should be discussed carefully with a tax consultant.

Maybe you're thinking that you couldn't possibly adopt because you already have biological children or because your children are nearly grown. I have met a number of women who have shared with me deep feelings of regret, saying, "I wish I had that third baby," or "that fourth," or "We talked about adoption, but we never did it."

At Orphans Overseas we do not have an age limit for adoptive parents unless an international country has set legal restrictions. We believe that if parents are healthy, even if they are older, they have much to offer a child. Some older parents have decided to raise a second family. While one spouse's parental longings may not be shared or even understood by the other, still that partner can make a decision to adopt, based on his or her desire to bring honor to Christ by loving a child who is precious to him.

The story is told of an old man walking down the beach who came across a section of sand obliterated by thousands of starfish which had been washed up by the waves. Knowing they would die if they didn't get back into the water soon, he began the laborious process of bending down and picking them up, one at a time, then heaving them back into the surf. Continuing his painstaking process, he was met by a passerby who stood and watched him momentarily, assessing the situation.

Observing the old man persevering in his overwhelming task, the passerby called out, "Why bother? You can't possibly make any difference!"

As if he had not heard the comment, the old man reached back down, almost reverently picking up another starfish. As he gently tossed it into the ocean he exclaimed, "It sure made a difference to this one!"

We may not be able to help every forgotten child by providing an adoptive family for him or her. But we can make an amazing difference to the ones we *can* find homes for. I am an example of one for whom adoption made a huge difference. Because I have seen a glimpse of the immense number of children in the world who are without parents, like Martin Luther King, Jr., I, too, have a dream. If *every* family could find enough love in their hearts to adopt just *one,* we could virtually wipe out the need for orphanages around the world.

Giving to Help Children

Still, some individuals will realize that for them, adoption is impossible. How can these individuals or families who are unable to adopt make a difference in the life or lives of children who otherwise may be forgotten? Reputable humanitarian organizations concentrating on orphans need our support. Our giving is multiplied because dollars have much buying power in a developing nation. A teacher may be employed in an orphanage at $60 U.S. per month in some places. In another country, $6,000 U.S. built a three-floor orphanage. When private humanitarian organizations partner with international governments to fund care programs in orphanages, much can be accomplished. Sponsoring schooling and basic needs for specific orphans and volunteering time to work with parentless children are also effective ways for people to make a difference. Becoming foster parents and temporarily providing a solid family for a child within one's own country is another way to significantly enrich a child's life.

Prayer

Some people will not be able to adopt or to give. What can they do? They can pray. For what?

* For the children who need parents in every country in the world.

* For birth parents who are unable to provide the kind of care they want for their children.

* For caregivers who are doing their best to stretch their resources and their love among too many children.

* For adoption laws in every country to facilitate efficient adoptions, making it possible for children to get to their new homes as soon as possible.

* For thousands of families to respond to the challenge to open their hearts and homes to children who need parents.

For a Child Like Valerie

Several of our agency staff attended a historic gathering marking the first adoptions ever completed in that country. Official government representatives, orphanage directors, and caregivers for the first four children who were to be placed for adoption sat in chairs lining the walls and in rows in the center of the room.

The mood was more somber than festive as caregivers sat with arms encircling these children for whom they had been responsible and to whom they now faced saying goodby. We had all shared tea together in the hosting orphanage's dining room. Now there were speeches to be given and farewells to be said before departing for our train, the first leg of our journey to the United States.

I was told that it would be appropriate for me to speak. As parting words were spoken by officials, I could see the mood becoming more and more mournful. These people loved the children—that was apparent. Separation was going to be difficult for both for the children and the staff. How could it be easy? The staff had a nearly impossible task. They had done their best to prepare the children for life in a country to which they had most likely never been—and for an adoptive relationship about which they knew very little.

Some of the individuals looked downhearted. Some of them looked angry, perhaps even hostile. I wondered what I could say to help them to understand adoption as I know it to be— a wonderful gift of a family to a child who would not otherwise have one. I did not want them to think that I didn't appreciate the good job they had done with these children. They had given of themselves to build strong relationships with the children, and it showed. But no matter how close a relationship can be with teachers or caregivers, they simply cannot substitute for a mother and father. I pondered what I could say. Too soon I was motioned to speak.

I started to stand and was motioned to stay sitting, so I did. I began with a story about adoption drawing us together, heart to heart. I did not think anyone was listening, judging by downcast eyes.

As I continued to speak, wondering what I could say that would build a bond between us, the youngest of the four children to be adopted, a three-year-old with a prosthesis on her leg, quietly slid down off the lap of the caregiver who held her and slowly began walking toward me from across the room. I saw Valerie from out of the corner of my eye; I thought, *What is she doing?* I continued speaking, though I could tell that she had diverted most everyone's attention.

When she got to me, her intentions became obvious. She crawled up into my lap, looked up at me and smiled! Hugging her while she played happily with my bracelet, I continued speaking. Now I knew what to say. My illustration sat in my lap.

"This is what I mean when I said adoption brings people heart to heart," I emphasized. "When you allow us to adopt your children, our countries have a bond that they never had before. When you allow us to adopt your children, we become family. And family is bonded forever. Before today we did not know each other. When we leave here today, we will part as family."

Before finishing, I noticed tears were starting to flow freely in that room. We exchanged emotional hugs, and our time together ended only because some of us needed to catch a train.

Did my words make a difference? I believe to this day that

on their own my words would have been ineffective. Why did little Valerie come to me that day? No one will ever know. She could not have known a word of English. My words must have sounded strange, and I was a total stranger to her. But her actions proved, with a clarity no words could have matched, that adoption brings people together. Because of a three-year-old girl, who was perhaps guided by the hand of an angel, everyone in that room that day witnessed the drawing together of people across cultures and oceans as only adoption can do. When concerned people work together, no children need to be forgotten.

Notes

Chapter 2: Forgotten Children
[1]*Characteristics of Children in Substitute and Adoptive Care,* The Voluntary Cooperative Information System, American Public Welfare Association, Washington, D.C., 1996.
[2]Ibid.
[3]George A. Akerlof and Janet L. Yellen, "New Mothers, Not Married," *The Brookings Review* (Fall 1996), pp. 19-21.
[4]June Ring, "The Church's Response to an Adoption-Resisting Culture," *Presbyterians Pro-Life NEWS* (Spring 1996).

Chapter 3: Is Adoption Second-Best?
[1]Billie Wilcox, "Lessons of Disaster," *Reader's Digest,* January 1980, p. 136.

Chapter 6: Genetic, Medical and Emotional Factors
[1]Peter L. Benson, Ph.D., Anu R. Sharma, Ph.D., L.P., Eugene C. Roehlkepartain, *Growing Up Adopted—A Portrait of Adolescents & Their Families* (Minneapolis, Minn.: Search Institute, 1994), p. 67.
[2]The Attachment Center at Evergreen. *Packet on Attachment Disorder.* Evergreen, Colorado. For more information, contact P.O. Box 2764, Evergreen, CO 80437-2764.

Chapter 8: Adopting the Older Child
[1]Benjamin Bloom, quoted by Jorie Kincaid, *The Power of Modeling, Hope for the Imperfect Parent* (Colorado Springs, Colo.: NavPress, 1989), p. 53.
[2]Harvard University's Preschool Project, quoted by Jorie Kincaid, *The Power of Modeling, Hope for the Imperfect Parent,* pp. 53, 67-68.

Chapter 10: Issues in Domestic Adoption in the U.S.
[1]George A. Akerlof and Janet L. Yellen, "New Mothers, Not Married," *The Brookings Review* (Fall 1996), pp. 19-21.
[2]Alec Grey, "Birthfathers and Legal Risks," *Adoptive Families* (March-April

1996), p. 20.

[3]Ibid. The National Adoption Information Clearinghouse (NAIC) has a fact sheet titled "Legal Issues of Independent Adoption" (1996, 14 pages). Contact NAIC at 5640 Nicholson Lane, Ste. 300, Rockville, MN 20852.

[4]Bill Keane, "The Family Circus," *The Oregonian,* Cowles Syndicate, Inc., October 10, 1993.

Chapter 11: Parenting the Adopted Child

[1]Some Scripture passages that speak about God's concern for orphans are as follows: Exodus 22:22; Deuteronomy 10:18; 16:11, 14; 24:17, 19; 26:12-13; 27:19; Job 29:12; 31:17, 21; Psalms 10:14, 18; 68:5; 82:3; 94:6; 146:9; Proverbs 23:10; Isaiah 1:17, 23; Jeremiah 5:28; 7:6; 22:3; 49:11; Ezekiel 22:7; Hosea 14:3; Zechariah 7:10; Malachi 3:5; James 1:27.

[2]William J. Gaither, Gloria Gaither, "I'm Something Special," Gaither Music Company, 1974. Used by permission.

Further Resources

Adoption Laws, Specific Countries
Brochures describing the adoption process and laws in many different countries are available from
Office of Children's Issues
Bureau of Consular Affairs
U.S. State Department
CA/OCS/CI, Room 4811, Department of State
Washington, DC 20520-4818
202-647-2680
Fax: 202-647-2835

Travel warnings, public announcements and consular information sheets on separate countries are available by automated fax for callers with a fax machine equipped with telephone. Contact
Office of Children's Issues
202-647-3000

For information on international adoption, specific-country adoption or foreign travel:
Website: http://travel.state.gov

U.S. Federal and State Adoption Laws; U.S. Adoption Agencies
The National Adoption Information Clearinghouse (NAIC) was established by Congress in 1987 as a service of the Administration on Children, Youth and Families in the U.S. Department of Health and Human Services. It offers
• personal answers to questions regarding adoption
• publications: directories list adoption information on agencies, support groups, training programs, media listings, crisis pregnancy centers
• library—open to the public
• referrals to adoption experts
• state and federal adoption laws
• catalog of audiovisual materials

National Adoption Information Clearinghouse
P.O. Box 1182
Washington, DC 20013-1182
703-352-3488 or 888-251-0075
Fax: 703-385-3206
E-mail: naic@calib.com
Website: http://www.calib.com/naic

Research, Opinion, Policy Documents re Adoption Issues
Adopt INFO: an electronic collection of research, opinion and policy documents related to issues facing adoptive families
   Website: http://www.cyfc.umn.edu/AdoptINFO.htp

Children, Youth and Family Consortium
12 McNeal Hall
1985 Buford Ave.
University of Minnesota
St. Paul, MN 55108
E-mail: cyfcec@maroon.tc.umn.edu

Independent Adoption
For information regarding legal issues pertinent to independent adoption (adoption not affiliated with an agency), "Legal Issues of Independent Adoption" (1996, 14 pages) is available from
   NAIC
   5640 Nicholson Lane, Ste. 300
   Rockville, MN 20852
   301-231-6512
   Fax: 301-984-8527

Immigrant Visas
U.S. citizens: For information on obtaining immigrant visas for internationally adopted children to gain entrance into their parents' country of residence, contact
   U.S. State Department Visa Office
   202-663-1225

For recorded information to request Immigrant Visa Application forms, contact
   U.S. Immigration and Naturalization Services (INS)
   1-800-870-FORM (3676)

To request Affadavit of Support forms, contact
   Bureau of Consular Affairs
   Autofax Service 202-647-3000
   Website: http://travel.state.gov/visa_services.html

U.S. citizens living abroad and citizens of international countries: Any child adopted in an intercountry adoption will need an immigrant visa to allow entrance into the new family's country of residence. American citizens living outside the U.S. and families who are citizens of another country must check with their country of residence to obtain a proper immigrant visa for an intercountry adoption.

Authentication of U.S. Documents

For U.S. federal authentication on documents for intercountry adoptions in countries not affiliated with the Hague Convention, contact

U.S. Department of State Authentications Office
2400 M St. N.W., Room 101
Washington, DC 20520
$4 per document for federal seals

Medical Resources for Adoptive Families

General Information:

International Adoption Clinic
University of Minnesota
Box 391
420 Delaware St. S.E.
Minneapolis, MN 55455
612-626-2928

Adoption/Medical News
551 Second Street
Ann Arbor, MI 48103
313-668-0419
E-mail: jajenista@mem.po.com

Hepatitis B:

Hepatitis B Foundation, a volunteer nonprofit organization, provides free educational materials about hepatitis B, including brochures, referrals, support groups.

101 Greenwood Ave. Suite 570
Jenkintown, PA 19046
215-884-8786
Fax: 215-887-1931
E-mail: hep-b@libertynet.org
Website: http://www.libertynet.org/~hep-b

Fetal Alcohol:

"Fetal Alcohol Syndrome: Diagnosis, Epidemiology, Prevention and Treatment' (Congress-mandated study by the National Institute on Alcohol Abuse and Alcoholism) available from

National Technical Information Service
703-487-4650

Attachment Disorder:
The Attachment Center at Evergreen
P.O. Box 2764
Evergreen, CO 80437-2764
303-674-1910
Fax: 303-670-3983

Adoption Financial Assistance:
"IRS Publication 968: Tax Benefits for Adoption" available from
National Adoption Information Clearinghouse
888-251-0075 or 703-352-3488
E-mail: [6] naic@calib.com

National Adoption Assistance Training, Resource and Information Network (NAA-TRIN), which is a program of the North American Council on Adoptable Children (NACAC), will provide preliminary information about adoption subsidies and other kinds of assistance. This number can also tell you how to reach your state's NAATRIN expert.
NAATRIN
1-800-470-6665

Author:
To reach the author of *Adopting for Good*, Jorie Kincaid, or for information regarding the agency with which she works, contact
Orphans Overseas
10226 S.W. Parkway
Portland, OR 97225
503-297-2006
Fax: 503-292-1258
E-mail: Orphanso@teleport com